Language: Usage and Practice, Grade 6

Contents

Introduction.. 3
Skills Correlation.. 5
Assessment.. 7

Unit 1: Vocabulary

Synonyms and Antonyms	11
Homonyms	12
Homographs	13
Prefixes	14
Suffixes	15
Contractions	16
Compound Words	17
Connotation/Denotation	18
Idioms	19
Unit 1 Test	20

Unit 2: Sentences

Recognizing Sentences	22
Types of Sentences	23
More Types of Sentences	24
Complete Subjects and Predicates	25
Simple Subjects and Predicates	26
Subjects and Predicates in Inverted Order	27
Using Compound Subjects	28
Using Compound Predicates	29
Simple and Compound Sentences	30
Correcting Run-on Sentences	31
Expanding Sentences	32
Unit 2 Test	33

Unit 3: Grammar and Usage

Nouns	35
Common and Proper Nouns	36
Singular and Plural Nouns	38
Possessive Nouns	40
Appositives	42
Verbs	43
Verb Phrases	44
Helping Verbs	45
More Helping Verbs	46
Using *Is/Are* and *Was/Were*	47
Verb Tenses	48
Principal Parts of Verbs	49
Past Tenses of *See, Do,* and *Come*	50
Past Tenses of *Eat* and *Drink*	51
Past Tenses of *Sing* and *Ring*	52
Past Tenses of *Freeze, Choose, Speak,* and *Break*	53
Past Tenses of *Know, Grow,* and *Throw*	54
Past Tenses of *Blow* and *Fly*	55
Past Tenses of *Take* and *Write*	56
Past Tenses of *Give* and *Go*	57
Possessive Pronouns	58
Indefinite Pronouns	59
Subject Pronouns	60
Object Pronouns	61
Subject Pronouns After Linking Verbs	62
Using *Who/Whom*	63
Using Pronouns	64
More Pronouns	65
Adjectives	66
Articles	67
Proper Adjectives	68
Demonstrative Adjectives	69

Contents continued

Contents continued

Comparing with Adjectives 70
More Comparing with Adjectives 71
Adverbs 73
Comparing with Adverbs 75
Using *Doesn't* and *Don't* 76
Using *May/Can* and *Teach/Learn* 77
Using *Sit/Set* and *Lie/Lay* 78
Prepositions 79
Prepositional Phrases 80
Prepositional Phrases as
   Adjectives/Adverbs 81
Conjunctions 82
Interjections 83
Unit 3 Test 84

Unit 4: Capitalization and Punctuation

Using Capital Letters 86
Using End Punctuation 89
Using Commas 91
Using Quotation Marks and
   Apostrophes 93
Using Colons and Hyphens 94
Unit 4 Test 95

Unit 5: Composition

Writing Sentences 97
Writing Topic Sentences 98
Writing Supporting Details 99
Topic and Audience 100
Taking Notes 101
Outlining 102
Writing a Report 103
Revising and Proofreading 104
Writing a Business Letter 106
Unit 5 Test 108

Unit 6: Study Skills

Dictionary: Guide Words 110
Dictionary: Syllables 111
Dictionary: Definitions and Parts
   of Speech 112
Dictionary: Word Origins 113
Using the Library 114
Using an Encyclopedia 115
Finding an Encyclopedia Article 116
Choosing Reference Sources 117
Unit 6 Test 118

Answer Key 120
Language Terms .... Inside Back Cover

Introduction

The *Language: Usage and Practice* series meets many needs.

- It is designed for students who require additional practice in the basics of effective writing and speaking.
- It provides focused practice in key grammar, usage, mechanics, and composition areas.
- It helps students gain ownership of essential skills.
- It presents practice exercises in a clear, concise format in a logical sequence.
- It allows for easy and independent use.

The *Language: Usage and Practice* lessons are organized into a series of units arranged in a logical sequence.

- vocabulary
- sentences
- grammar and usage
- mechanics of capitalization and punctuation
- composition skills

The *Language: Usage and Practice* lessons are carefully formatted for student comfort.

- Systematic, focused attention is given to just one carefully selected skill at a time.
- Rules are clearly stated at the beginning of each lesson and are illustrated with examples.
- Key terms are introduced in bold type.
- Meaningful practice exercises reinforce the skill.
- Each lesson is clearly labeled, and directions are clear and uncomplicated.

The *Language: Usage and Practice* series stresses the application of language principles in a variety of ways.

- Students are asked to match, circle, or underline elements in a predetermined sentence.
- Students are also asked to use what they have learned in an original sentence or in rewriting a sentence.

The *Language: Usage and Practice* series is designed for independent use.

- Because the format is logical and consistent and the vocabulary is carefully controlled, students can use *Language: Usage and Practice* with a high degree of independence.
- Copies of the worksheets can be given to individuals, pairs of students, or small groups for completion.
- Worksheets can be used in the language arts center.
- Worksheets can be given as homework for reviewing and reinforcing skills.

The *Language: Usage and Practice* series provides writing instruction.

- The process approach to teaching writing provides success for most students.
- *Language: Usage and Practice* provides direct support for the teaching of composition and significantly enhances those strategies and techniques commonly associated with the process-writing approach.
- Each book includes a composition unit that provides substantial work with composition skills, such as writing topic sentences, selecting supporting details, taking notes, writing reports, and revising and proofreading.
- Also included in the composition unit is practice with various prewriting activities, such as clustering and brainstorming, which play an important part in process writing.
- The composition lessons are presented in the same rule-plus-practice format as in the other units.

The *Language: Usage and Practice* series includes additional features.

- **Unit Tests**   Use the unit tests to check student progress and prepare students for standardized tests.
- **Sequential Support**   The content of each unit is repeated and expanded in subsequent levels as highlighted in the skills correlation chart on pages 5 and 6.
- **Assessment**   Use the Assessment on pages 7–10 to determine the skills your students need to practice.
- **Language Terms**   Provide each student with a copy of the list of language terms on the inside back cover to keep for reference throughout the year.
- **Small-Group Activities**   Use the worksheets as small-group activities to give students the opportunity to work cooperatively.

The *Language: Usage and Practice* series is a powerful tool!

The activities use a variety of strategies to maintain student interest.
Watch your students' language improve as skills are
applied in structured, relevant practice!

Skills Correlation

	1	2	3	4	5	6	7	8	High School
Vocabulary									
Rhyming Words	■	■							
Synonyms and Antonyms	■	■	■	■	■	■	■	■	■
Homonyms	■	■	■	■	■	■	■	■	■
Multiple Meanings/Homographs	■	■	■	■	■	■	■	■	■
Prefixes and Suffixes			■	■	■	■	■	■	■
Compound Words			■	■	■	■	■	■	■
Contractions			■	■	■	■	■	■	■
Idioms						■	■	■	■
Connotation/Denotation					■	■	■	■	
Sentences									
Word Order in Sentences	■	■		■					
Recognizing Sentences and Sentence Types	■	■	■	■	■	■	■	■	■
Subjects and Predicates	■	■	■	■	■	■	■	■	■
Compound/Complex Sentences			■	■	■	■	■	■	■
Sentence Combining			■	■	■	■	■	■	■
Run-on Sentences			■	■	■	■	■	■	■
Independent and Subordinate Clauses						■	■	■	■
Compound Subjects and Predicates	■			■	■	■	■	■	■
Direct and Indirect Objects					■		■	■	■
Inverted Word Order						■	■	■	■
Grammar and Usage									
Common and Proper Nouns	■	■	■	■	■	■	■	■	■
Singular and Plural Nouns	■	■	■	■	■	■	■	■	■
Possessive Nouns			■	■	■	■	■	■	■
Appositives						■	■	■	
Verbs and Verb Tense	■	■	■	■	■	■	■	■	■
Regular/Irregular Verbs	■	■	■	■	■	■	■	■	■
Subject/Verb Agreement	■	■	■	■	■	■	■	■	■
Verb Phrases						■	■	■	■
Transitive and Intransitive Verbs							■	■	
Verbals: Gerunds, Participles, and Infinitives							■	■	■
Active and Passive Voice							■	■	
Mood								■	
Pronouns	■	■	■	■	■	■	■	■	■
Antecedents					■		■	■	■
Articles	■	■	■		■	■			
Adjectives	■	■	■	■	■	■	■	■	■
Correct Word Usage (e.g., may/can, sit/set)	■		■	■	■	■	■	■	■
Adverbs			■	■	■	■	■	■	■
Prepositions						■	■	■	■
Prepositional Phrases						■	■	■	■
Conjunctions						■	■	■	■
Interjections						■	■		
Double Negatives								■	■
Capitalization and Punctuation									
Capitalization: First Word in Sentence	■	■	■	■	■	■	■	■	■
Capitalization: Proper Nouns	■	■	■	■	■	■	■	■	■
Capitalization: in Letters			■	■	■		■	■	■
Capitalization: Abbreviations and Titles			■	■	■	■	■	■	■
Capitalization: Proper Adjectives					■	■	■	■	■

	1	2	3	4	5	6	7	8	High School
Capitalization and Punctuation (cont'd)									
End Punctuation	■	■	■	■	■	■	■	■	■
Commas		■	■	■	■	■	■	■	■
Apostrophes in Contractions		■	■	■	■	■	■	■	■
Apostrophes in Possessives			■	■	■	■	■	■	■
Quotation Marks			■	■	■	■	■	■	■
Colons/Semicolons					■	■	■	■	■
Hyphens						■	■	■	■
Composition									
Expanding Sentences			■		■	■	■	■	
Paragraphs: Topic Sentence (main idea)		■	■	■	■	■	■	■	■
Paragraphs: Supporting Details		■	■	■	■	■	■	■	■
Order in Paragraphs			■	■	■	■	■		■
Writing Process:									
Audience				■	■	■	■	■	
Topic			■	■	■	■	■	■	
Outlining				■		■	■	■	
Clustering/Brainstorming					■		■	■	
Note Taking						■			
Revising/Proofreading					■	■	■	■	
Types of Writing:									
Poem	■								
Letter	■	■	■			■			
"How-to" Paragraph				■					
Invitation				■					
Telephone Message				■					
Conversation					■				
Narrative Paragraph					■				
Comparing and Contrasting						■			
Descriptive Paragraph						■			
Report						■			
Interview							■		
Persuasive Composition								■	
Readiness/Study Skills									
Grouping	■		■						
Letters of Alphabet	■								
Listening	■	■							
Making Comparisons	■	■							
Organizing Information			■	■					
Following Directions	■	■	■	■	■				
Alphabetical Order	■	■	■	■	■				
Using a Dictionary:									
Definitions		■	■			■	■	■	
Guide Words/Entry Words		■	■	■	■	■	■	■	
Syllables and Pronunciation					■	■	■	■	
Multiple Meanings		■	■			■	■	■	
Word Origins						■	■	■	
Parts of a Book		■				■			
Using the Library						■	■	■	
Using Encyclopedias				■	■	■	■	■	
Using Reference Books						■	■	■	
Using the *Readers' Guide*							■	■	
Using Tables, Charts, Graphs, and Diagrams								■	
Choosing Appropriate Sources						■	■	■	

Name _____ Date _____

Assessment

❋ Write **S** before each pair of synonyms, **A** before each pair of antonyms, and **H** before each pair of homonyms.

_____ 1. full, empty

_____ 2. lead, led

_____ 3. journal, notebook

_____ 4. would, wood

❋ Write the homograph for the pair of meanings.

5. _____ **a.** a container   **b.** to be able

❋ Write **P** before each word with a prefix, **S** before each word with a suffix, and **C** before each compound word.

_____ 6. joyous

_____ 7. outcome

_____ 8. disappear

_____ 9. mislead

❋ Write the words that make up each contraction.

10. can't _____ _____

11. they'll _____ _____

❋ Underline the word in parentheses that has the more positive connotation.

12. Our (nosy, curious) neighbor peeked over the fence.

❋ Circle the letter of the idiom that means out of favor.

13. **a.** down in the dumps   **b.** in the doghouse

❋ Write **D** before the declarative sentence, **IM** before the imperative sentence, **E** before the exclamatory sentence, and **IN** before the interrogative sentence. Then circle the simple subject and underline the simple predicate in each sentence.

_____ 14. Who is going with us?

_____ 15. I feel awful!

_____ 16. Don't worry about a thing.

_____ 17. It is best just to wait.

❋ Write **CS** before the sentence that has a compound subject. Write **CP** before the sentence that has a compound predicate.

_____ 18. The dog growled and barked.

_____ 19. Broccoli and carrots are tasty vegetables.

❋ Write **CS** before the compound sentence. Write **RO** before the run-on sentence. Write **I** before the sentence that is in inverted order.

_____ 20. We had been there once before, it was familiar to me.

_____ 21. Around the corner sped the getaway car.

_____ 22. Time was running out, and darkness was falling.

❋ Underline the common nouns and circle the proper nouns in the sentence.

23. The police officer told Paul that Judge Hawkins was the person who would decide.

---

www.harcourtschoolsupply.com

© Harcourt Achieve Inc. All rights reserved.

Assessment
Language: Usage and Practice 6, SV 1419027832

Name _____ Date _____

Assessment, p. 2

Write the correct possessive noun to complete the second sentence.

24. The car of her friend was stolen. Her _____ car was stolen.

Underline the appositive in the sentence. Circle the noun it identifies or explains.

25. Nolan Ryan, a baseball legend, is signing autographs at the store.

Underline the verb phrase and circle the helping verb.

26. He will soon discover the error in his plan.

Write past, present, or future to show the tense of each underlined verb.

_____ 27. Yesterday it rained very hard.

_____ 28. Soon the clouds will disappear.

_____ 29. Sunny days are my favorite.

Circle the correct verbs in parentheses to complete each sentence.

30. Rosa (fly, flew) to Paris and (went, gone) to see the Eiffel Tower.

31. She (drink, drank) the soda and (throw, threw) the can in the recycling bin.

32. The ice (frozen, froze) hard but (broke, broken) up in the spring.

Write SP before the sentence that has a subject pronoun, OP before the sentence that has an object pronoun, PP before the sentence that has a possessive pronoun, and IP before the sentence that has an indefinite pronoun. Circle the pronoun in each sentence.

_____ 33. You should take a nap.

_____ 34. Nobody knew what happened.

_____ 35. A smile was her answer.

_____ 36. Frank didn't even hear us.

On the line before each sentence, write adjective or adverb to describe the underlined word.

_____ 37. These are my favorite books.

_____ 38. He eats here regularly.

_____ 39. You are too hasty.

_____ 40. She is an actor.

Circle the correct word in parentheses to complete each sentence.

41. (May, Can) you see from here?

42. You must (teach, learn) to be patient.

43. Just (sit, set) your shoes over there.

44. She (lied, laid) down the book.

45. He (doesn't, don't) want to go.

Name _____ Date _____

Assessment, p. 3

✻ **Underline each prepositional phrase twice. Circle each preposition. Underline the conjunctions once.**

46. You can wait either in the car or outside the door.

✻ **Rewrite the letter. Use capital letters and punctuation marks where needed.**

                                      832 southern star
                                      helena mt 95097
                                      aug 27 2007

dear edward

    i have the information you wanted ____ did you ever think id get it to you this quickly ____ well its time i surprised you ____ heres what you should bring six cartons of orange juice forty five paper cups and three bags of ice ____ what a breakfast party this will be ____

                                        your friend
                                        bill

_____

_____

_____

_____

_____

_____

_____

_____

_____

_____

✻ **Write a topic sentence and two sentences with descriptive supporting details on the topic of home safety.**

47. _____

_____

_____

Name _____ Date _____

Assessment, p. 4

Number the steps for writing a report in order.

_____ **48.** Write the report.

_____ **49.** Organize your research questions.

_____ **50.** Revise and proofread your report.

_____ **51.** Look in an encyclopedia.

_____ **52.** Write information in your own words.

_____ **53.** Make an outline.

Circle the part that does <u>not</u> belong in a business letter.

54. heading   closing   title   signature   body   greeting

Use the dictionary entry below to answer the questions.

carpet (kär′ pit) *n.* **1.** a thick floor covering; rug: *She cleaned the carpet.*
2. a surface like a rug: *A carpet of leaves covered the ground.*

55. What part of speech is the word <u>carpet</u>? _____

56. Would <u>carport</u> come before or after <u>carpet</u> in the dictionary? _____

57. Would <u>cart/cast</u> or <u>care/carrot</u> be the guide words for <u>carpet</u>? _____

58. Write the number of the definition for <u>carpet</u> in this sentence: The fawn lay on a carpet of grass. _____

59. Write <u>carpet</u> separated into syllables. _____

Write the source from the box that you would use to find the information listed.

dictionary   encyclopedia   atlas

_____ **60.** a map of the world

_____ **61.** an article on Africa

_____ **62.** how to divide a word

_____ **63.** where the mouth of the Mississippi River is

_____ **64.** the meaning of a word

_____ **65.** information about Abraham Lincoln

Name _____ Date _____

Synonyms and Antonyms

- A **synonym** is a word that has the same or nearly the same meaning as one or more other words.
  EXAMPLES: joy—happiness   choose—pick

 Write a synonym for each word below.

1. small _____
2. swiftly _____
3. wear _____
4. pretty _____
5. large _____
6. awful _____
7. lad _____
8. forest _____
9. cry _____
10. leap _____
11. wealthy _____
12. ugly _____

 Circle the word in parentheses that is a synonym for the underlined word in each sentence.

13. (finish, begin)   When you start to write, think about your audience.
14. (fall, spring)   The colors of autumn leaves are breathtaking.
15. (sick, well)   Last week I was ill with the flu.
16. (tried, tired)   He was exhausted after the marathon.
17. (clothes, close)   I tried to shut the door, but it was stuck.

- An **antonym** is a word that has the opposite meaning of another word.
  EXAMPLES: hot—cold   late—early

 Write an antonym for each word below.

18. good _____
19. old _____
20. dull _____
21. thick _____
22. tall _____
23. crooked _____
24. happy _____
25. remember _____
26. ugly _____
27. near _____
28. obey _____
29. rich _____

 Circle the word in parentheses that is an antonym for the underlined word in each sentence.

30. (heavy, hard)   The donkey strained under its light load.
31. (last, late)   The early morning sun streamed in the window.
32. (fine, kind)   Jay gave the dog a mean pat on the head.
33. (empty, old)   I tried to pour some milk, but the carton was full.
34. (frowned, found)   Isabel lost her favorite book.

Name _____   Date _____

Homonyms

- A **homonym** is a word that sounds the same as another word but has a different spelling and a different meaning.
  EXAMPLES: to—two—too   sum—some

 Underline the correct homonym(s) in each sentence below.

1. The couple walked for a mile along the (beech, beach).
2. Are there any (dear, deer) in these hills?
3. How much do you (way, weigh)?
4. Who broke this (pane, pain) in the window?
5. I have (to, too, two) go (to, too, two) the sale with those (to, too, two) people.
6. Lori (knew, new) how to play a (new, knew) word game.
7. Juan and Luis spent a week at (there, their) friends' ranch.
8. Those boys (ate, eight) (ate, eight) of the apples we had just bought.
9. I like to walk by the (see, sea) at dusk.
10. (Wring, Ring) the bell, Matt.
11. Did you see what she brought (hear, here)?
12. He cannot (write, right) with his (write, right) hand.
13. Who has not (read, red) the magazine?
14. He found it cheaper to (buy, by) his pencils (buy, by) the box.
15. Chris told his niece a fairy (tale, tail).

 Write a homonym for each word below.

16. hall _____
17. threw _____
18. weak _____
19. there _____
20. heard _____
21. here _____
22. by _____
23. pane _____
24. heal _____
25. blew _____

26. flower _____
27. stair _____
28. pale _____
29. ring _____
30. soar _____
31. sale _____
32. won _____
33. aisle _____
34. rode _____
35. meet _____

36. our _____
37. sea _____
38. right _____
39. peace _____
40. no _____
41. grate _____
42. way _____
43. cent _____
44. dew _____
45. forth _____

Name _____   Date _____

Homographs

- A **homograph** is a word that has the same spelling as another word but a different meaning and sometimes a different pronunciation.
  EXAMPLE: **bow**, meaning "to bend the upper part of the body forward in respect," and **bow**, meaning "a weapon for shooting arrows"

| vault | checks | interest |

Complete each sentence with a homograph from the box. Use each homograph twice.

1. With a bank account, you can write _____ to pay for things.

2. She looked with great _____ at the painting.

3. He used a long pole to _____ over the jump.

4. My savings account pays _____ on the money I keep in it.

5. Jesse keeps his stamp collection locked in a _____.

6. She wrote small _____ beside each item on the list.

Circle the letter of the correct definition for each underlined homograph. Then write a sentence using the other meaning of the homograph.

7. Put your coins in the <u>bank</u>.
   a. a place where people save money   b. the ground along a river
   _____

8. If you <u>hide</u> your bank, be sure to remember where you put it.
   a. keep out of sight   b. the skin of an animal
   _____

9. Some people keep their money in a <u>safe</u>.
   a. a metal box with a lock   b. free from danger
   _____

10. There are only two people who have the <u>key</u> to open the safe.
    a. a piece of metal to open a lock   b. a low island or reef
    _____

11. Many people have an <u>account</u> at a bank.
    a. explanation   b. an amount of money
    _____

Unit 1: Vocabulary
Language: Usage and Practice 6, SV 1419027832

Name _____ Date _____

Prefixes

- A **prefix** added to the beginning of a base word changes the meaning of the word.
    EXAMPLE: <u>un</u>, meaning "not," + the base word <u>done</u> = <u>undone</u>, meaning "not done"
- Some prefixes have one meaning, and others have more than one meaning.
    EXAMPLES

prefix	meaning
im, in, non, un	not
dis, in, non	opposite of, lack of, not
mis	bad, badly, wrong, wrongly
pre	before
re	again

 Add the prefix <u>un</u>, <u>im</u>, <u>non</u>, or <u>mis</u> to the base word in parentheses. Write the new word in the sentence. Then write the definition of the new word on the line after the sentence. Use a dictionary if necessary.

1. It is _____ (practical) to put a new monkey into a cage with other monkeys.
_____

2. The monkeys might _____ (behave) with a newcomer among them.
_____

3. They will also feel quite _____ (easy) for a number of days or even weeks.
_____

4. Even if the new monkey is _____ (violent) in nature, the others may harm it.
_____

5. Sometimes animal behavior can be quite _____ (usual).
_____

 Underline each prefix. Write the meaning of each word that has a prefix.

6. unexpected guest _____

7. really disappear _____

8. disagree often _____

9. misspell a name _____

10. preview a movie _____

11. reenter a room _____

12. misplace a shoe _____

13. impossible situation _____

14. nonstop reading _____

15. unimportant discussion _____

16. insane story _____

17. prejudge a person _____

Name _____ Date _____

Suffixes

- A **suffix** added to the end of a base word changes the meaning of the word.
  EXAMPLE: <u>ful</u>, meaning "full of," + the base word <u>joy</u> = <u>joyful</u>, meaning "full of joy"
- Some suffixes have one meaning, and others have more than one meaning.
  EXAMPLES:

suffix	meaning
able	able to be, suitable, or inclined to
al	relating to, like
ful	as much as will fill, full of
less	without, that does not
ous	full of
y	having, full of

 Add a suffix from the list above to the base word in parentheses. Write the new word. Then write the definition of the new word on the line after the sentence. Do not use any suffix more than once.

1. Switzerland is a _____ country. (mountain)

   _____

2. If you visit there, it is _____ to have a walking stick. (help)

   _____

3. Many tourists visit the country's _____ mountains to ski each year. (snow)

   _____

4. The Swiss people have a great deal of _____ pride. (nation)

   _____

5. Many Swiss are _____ about their country's history. (knowledge)

   _____

Underline each suffix. Write the meaning of each word that has a suffix.

6. breakable toy _____

7. endless waves _____

8. hazardous path _____

9. inflatable raft _____

10. poisonous snake _____

11. dependable trains _____

12. humorous program _____

13. tearful good-bye _____

14. bumpy ride _____

15. careless driver _____

16. natural food _____

17. magical experience _____

Name _____ Date _____

Contractions

> - A **contraction** is a word formed by joining two other words.
> - An **apostrophe** (') shows where a letter or letters have been left out.
>   EXAMPLE: do not = don't
> - <u>Won't</u> is an exception.
>   EXAMPLE: will not = won't

 Underline each contraction. Write the words that make up each contraction on the line.

1. Stingrays look as if they're part bird, part fish. _____

2. Stingrays cover themselves with sand so they won't be seen. _____

3. There's a chance that a wader might step on a stingray and get stung. _____

4. That's a painful way to learn that you shouldn't forget about stingrays.

    _____   _____

5. Until recently, stingrays weren't seen very often. _____

6. It doesn't seem likely, but some stingrays will eat out of divers' hands. _____

7. Because its mouth is underneath, the stingray can't see what it's eating.

    _____   _____

8. Once they've been fed by hand, they'll flutter around for more.

    _____   _____

9. It's hard to believe these stingrays aren't afraid of humans.

    _____   _____

10. To pet a stingray, you'd gently touch its velvety skin. _____

 Find the pairs of words that can be made into contractions. Underline each pair. Then write the contraction each word pair can make on the lines following the sentences.

11. I have never tried scuba diving, but I would like to.

    _____   _____

12. It is a good way to explore what is under the water.

    _____   _____

13. First, I will need to take lessons in the pool. _____

14. Then I can find out what to do if the equipment does not work. _____

Name _____   Date _____

Compound Words

- A **compound word** is a word that is made up of two or more words.
- The meaning of a compound word is related to the meaning of each individual word.
  - EXAMPLE: sun + glasses = sunglasses, meaning "glasses to wear in the sun"
- Compound words may be written as one word, as hyphenated words, or as two separate words.
  - EXAMPLES: highway   high-rise   high school

 Answer the following questions.

1. Something that has sharp, curved points extending backward is said to be barbed.

   What is barbed wire? _____

2. Dry means "without water." What does dry-clean mean? _____

3. Head means "a heading." What is a headline? _____

4. A deputy is "a person appointed to take the place of another."

   What is a deputy marshal? _____

5. Bare means "without a covering." What does bareback mean? _____

6. A road is a route. What is a railroad? _____

7. A paper is a type of document. What is a newspaper? _____

8. Blue is a color. What is a blueberry? _____

 Combine words from the box to make compound words. Use the compound words to complete the sentences. You will use one word twice.

cut	every	fore	hair	head	where
loud	news	speaker	stand	thing	

9. Rob's hair covered his _____.

10. He knew it was time to get a _____.

11. He saw a truck hit a fire hydrant, which sprayed water _____.

12. The corner _____ was soaked.

13. A police officer used a _____.

14. It was so exciting that Rob forgot about _____, including his haircut!

Name _____ Date _____

Connotation/Denotation

- The **denotation** of a word is its exact meaning as stated in a dictionary.
  EXAMPLE: The denotation of skinny is "very thin."
- The connotation of a word is an added meaning that suggests something positive or negative.
  EXAMPLES:
  Negative: Skinny suggests "too thin." Skinny has a negative connotation.
  Positive: Slender suggests "attractively thin." Slender has a positive connotation.
- Some words are neutral. They do not suggest either good or bad feelings.
  EXAMPLES: month   building   chair

 Underline the word in parentheses that has the more positive connotation.

1. Our trip to the amusement park was (fine, wonderful).
2. (Brave, Foolhardy) people rode on the roller coaster.
3. We saw (fascinating, weird) animals in the animal house.
4. Some of the monkeys made (hilarious, amusing) faces.
5. Everyone had a (smile, smirk) on his or her face on the way home.

 Underline the word in parentheses that has the more negative connotation.

6. We bought (cheap, inexpensive) souvenirs at the amusement park.
7. I ate a (soggy, moist) sandwich.
8. Mike (nagged, reminded) us to go to the fun house.
9. The fun house was (comical, silly).
10. I didn't like the (smirk, grin) on the jester's face.
11. It made me feel (uneasy, frightened).

 Answer the following questions.

12. Which is worth more, something old or something antique? _____

13. Is it better to be slender or to be skinny? _____

14. Which would you rather be called, thrifty or cheap? _____

15. Would a vain person be more likely to stroll or to parade? _____

16. Which is more serious, a problem or a disaster? _____

17. Is it more polite to sip a drink or to gulp it? _____

18. If you hadn't eaten for days, would you be hungry or starving? _____

19. After walking in mud, would your shoes be dirty or filthy? _____

Name _____ Date _____

Idioms

> • An **idiom** is an expression that has a meaning different from the usual meanings of the individual words within it.
> EXAMPLE: To lend a hand means "to help," not "to loan someone a hand."

 Match the idioms underlined in the sentences below with their meanings. Write the letter of the correct answer on the line.

a. in a risky situation
b. do less than I should
c. admit having said the wrong thing
d. play music after only hearing it
e. spend money carefully

f. continue to have hope
g. listen with all your attention
h. teasing
i. accept defeat
j. meet by chance

_____ 1. I had hoped to run across some old friends at the ball game.

_____ 2. Their team was ready to throw in the towel when we scored our tenth run!

_____ 3. Angela was pulling my leg when she told me that there are koalas in Africa.

_____ 4. I told her that she was skating on thin ice when she tried to trick me.

_____ 5. My sister must make ends meet with the little money she has for college.

_____ 6. I told her, "Always keep your chin up when things get difficult."

_____ 7. Karl can play by ear the theme songs to all his favorite movies.

_____ 8. If you don't believe me, just be all ears when he plays.

_____ 9. My brother said that I would lie down on the job if he weren't watching over me.

_____ 10. I told Bill that he would eat his words once he saw how much work I had done.

Underline the idioms in the following sentences. On the line after each sentence, explain what the idiom means. Use a dictionary if necessary.

11. Frank was in hot water when he arrived late.

_____

12. His friends were beside themselves with worry.

_____

13. Frank told them not to fly off the handle.

_____

14. His friends explained that they had been shaken up.

_____

15. They all decided to sit down and talk turkey.

_____

Name _____ Date _____

Unit 1 Test

Decide whether the underlined words in each sentence are synonyms, antonyms, homonyms, or homographs. Darken the circle by your choice.

1. If you duck your head under here, you can see the baby duck.
   Ⓐ synonyms   Ⓑ antonyms   Ⓒ homonyms   Ⓓ homographs

2. Please show me how to operate the lawn mower, so I can use it properly.
   Ⓐ synonyms   Ⓑ antonyms   Ⓒ homonyms   Ⓓ homographs

3. My friend asked me a question, but I told him I didn't know the answer.
   Ⓐ synonyms   Ⓑ antonyms   Ⓒ homonyms   Ⓓ homographs

4. The perfume she sent has a wonderful scent.
   Ⓐ synonyms   Ⓑ antonyms   Ⓒ homonyms   Ⓓ homographs

5. Don't worry about something that's not real; nothing will come of it.
   Ⓐ synonyms   Ⓑ antonyms   Ⓒ homonyms   Ⓓ homographs

6. Even though its leg is hurt, it's not broken.
   Ⓐ synonyms   Ⓑ antonyms   Ⓒ homonyms   Ⓓ homographs

7. Can you reach that can of peaches on the top shelf?
   Ⓐ synonyms   Ⓑ antonyms   Ⓒ homonyms   Ⓓ homographs

8. The brave soldiers won their battle, and they won medals for their fearless deeds.
   Ⓐ synonyms   Ⓑ antonyms   Ⓒ homonyms   Ⓓ homographs

9. They're going to their cabin for vacation.
   Ⓐ synonyms   Ⓑ antonyms   Ⓒ homonyms   Ⓓ homographs

10. Before you begin the next topic, please let me finish taking notes on this one.
    Ⓐ synonyms   Ⓑ antonyms   Ⓒ homonyms   Ⓓ homographs

Add a prefix or suffix to the underlined word to make a new word that makes sense in the sentence. Darken the circle by your choice.

11. It is possible to sleep in at my house.
    Ⓐ pre   Ⓒ im
    Ⓑ un   Ⓓ ity

12. We spend end hours talking together.
    Ⓐ un   Ⓒ ful
    Ⓑ less   Ⓓ ous

13. Please move your shoes before entering.
    Ⓐ un   Ⓒ y
    Ⓑ able   Ⓓ re

14. Be care not to disturb the baby.
    Ⓐ ful   Ⓒ able
    Ⓑ less   Ⓓ mis

15. The train traveled stop to Chicago.
    Ⓐ dis   Ⓒ non
    Ⓑ able   Ⓓ mis

16. She had a remark way of explaining.
    Ⓐ un   Ⓒ ness
    Ⓑ able   Ⓓ mis

Unit 1 Test, p. 2

17. That country is very mountain.
- Ⓐ al
- Ⓑ ness
- Ⓒ able
- Ⓓ ous

18. He placed his new hat.
- Ⓐ un
- Ⓑ mis
- Ⓒ non
- Ⓓ able

19. We enjoyed the movie view.
- Ⓐ al
- Ⓑ dis
- Ⓒ pre
- Ⓓ un

20. We take an occasion trip.
- Ⓐ al
- Ⓑ ous
- Ⓒ un
- Ⓓ y

Darken the circle by the correct contraction for each pair of underlined words.

21. you would
- Ⓐ you'd
- Ⓑ you'ld
- Ⓒ y'oud
- Ⓓ youd'

22. they are
- Ⓐ there
- Ⓑ their
- Ⓒ theyr'e
- Ⓓ they're

23. it is
- Ⓐ its'
- Ⓑ it's
- Ⓒ ites
- Ⓓ its

24. will not
- Ⓐ win't
- Ⓑ wo'nt
- Ⓒ won't
- Ⓓ willn't

25. I will
- Ⓐ I'm
- Ⓑ I've
- Ⓒ I'll
- Ⓓ I'd

26. does not
- Ⓐ didn't
- Ⓑ doesn't
- Ⓒ don't
- Ⓓ does'nt

Add a word to each underlined word to make it a compound word. Darken the circle by your choice.

27. We took the ferry to the island.
- Ⓐ tale
- Ⓑ boat
- Ⓒ man
- Ⓓ route

28. She could not stand him.
- Ⓐ by
- Ⓑ head
- Ⓒ grand
- Ⓓ under

Choose whether each underlined word has a positive connotation (+), a negative connotation (−), or is neutral (N). Darken the circle by your choice.

29. This dress is cheap.   Ⓐ (+)   Ⓑ (−)   Ⓒ (N)

30. My sister is very slender.   Ⓐ (+)   Ⓑ (−)   Ⓒ (N)

31. Tom will walk with us.   Ⓐ (+)   Ⓑ (−)   Ⓒ (N)

32. The movie was disgusting.   Ⓐ (+)   Ⓑ (−)   Ⓒ (N)

33. The heroine was brave.   Ⓐ (+)   Ⓑ (−)   Ⓒ (N)

34. Did you ask your doctor?   Ⓐ (+)   Ⓑ (−)   Ⓒ (N)

Darken the circle by the correct meaning for each idiom.

35. beside herself
- Ⓐ out of favor
- Ⓑ very upset
- Ⓒ unable to decide
- Ⓓ in a difficult situation

36. walking on air
- Ⓐ ready to accept defeat
- Ⓑ extremely happy
- Ⓒ meet by chance
- Ⓓ in trouble

Name _____ Date _____

Recognizing Sentences

> • A **sentence** is a group of words that expresses a complete thought.
>   EXAMPLE: Marie sings well.

✳ **Some of the following groups of words are sentences, and some are not. Write S before each group that is a sentence. Punctuate each sentence with a period.**

_____ 1. When the downhill skiing season begins ____

_____ 2. Last summer I visited my friend in New Jersey ____

_____ 3. From the very beginning of the first-aid lessons ____

_____ 4. One of the children from the neighborhood ____

_____ 5. A visiting musician played the organ ____

_____ 6. On the way to school this morning ____

_____ 7. "I love you, Mother," said Pat ____

_____ 8. The blue house at the corner of Maple Street ____

_____ 9. After Emily left, the phone rang off the hook ____

_____ 10. Speak distinctly and loudly so that you can be heard ____

_____ 11. I have finally learned to drive our car ____

_____ 12. This is William's tenth birthday ____

_____ 13. At the very last moment, we were ready ____

_____ 14. When you speak in front of people ____

_____ 15. The basket of fruit on the table ____

_____ 16. Please answer the telephone, Julio ____

_____ 17. Hurrying to class because he is late ____

_____ 18. The first thing in the morning ____

_____ 19. That mistake was costly and unfortunate ____

_____ 20. We are planning to build a new doghouse ____

_____ 21. The dog chased the cat up the tree ____

_____ 22. Daniel Boone was born in Pennsylvania ____

_____ 23. The giant cottonwood in our backyard ____

_____ 24. Maria, bring my notebook ____

_____ 25. On a stool beside the back door ____

_____ 26. Sometimes the noise from the street ____

_____ 27. Somewhere out of state ____

_____ 28. The band played a lively march ____

_____ 29. That flight arrived on time ____

_____ 30. Was cracked in dozens of places ____

Types of Sentences

- A **declarative sentence** makes a statement. It is followed by a period (.).
    EXAMPLES: It is hot today. I took off my jacket.
- An **interrogative sentence** asks a question. It is followed by a question mark (?).
    EXAMPLES: When is Jason coming? Why is the bus late today?

Write D before each declarative sentence and IN before each interrogative sentence. Put the correct punctuation mark at the end of the sentence.

_____ 1. Who is your favorite author ____
_____ 2. How are our forests protected from fire ____
_____ 3. Vince learned the names of the trees in his neighborhood ____
_____ 4. A good driver obeys every traffic law ____
_____ 5. The hippopotamus lives in Africa ____
_____ 6. Do you know the legend of the dogwood tree ____
_____ 7. Every sentence should begin with a capital letter ____
_____ 8. Ryan is repairing the lamp ____
_____ 9. Did you ever see a kangaroo ____
_____ 10. Where did these fragrant roses grow ____
_____ 11. Beautiful furniture can be made from the oak tree ____
_____ 12. Flour can be made from dried bananas ____
_____ 13. Did anyone find Steve's book ____
_____ 14. Andrea feeds the goldfish every day ____
_____ 15. How many people are studying to be pilots ____
_____ 16. Kelly is going to the show with us ____
_____ 17. Last summer we made a trip to Carlsbad Caverns ____
_____ 18. How old are you ____
_____ 19. The architect and her assistant inspected the building ____
_____ 20. When did you arrive at the meeting ____
_____ 21. Did you forget your wallet ____
_____ 22. That lightbulb is burned out ____
_____ 23. The baby crawled across the room ____
_____ 24. When would you like to eat ____
_____ 25. Harrison helped Andy wash the car ____
_____ 26. Did they wax the car ____
_____ 27. How did you make that sand castle ____
_____ 28. It is easy to make if we work together ____

Name _____ Date _____

More Types of Sentences

> - An **imperative sentence** expresses a command or a request. It is followed by a period (.).
>   EXAMPLE: Close the door.
> - An **exclamatory sentence** expresses strong or sudden feeling. It is followed by an exclamation point (!).
>   EXAMPLE: I am innocent!

Write <u>IM</u> before each imperative sentence and <u>E</u> before each exclamatory sentence. Put the correct punctuation mark at the end of each sentence.

_____ 1. Write the names of the days of the week ____
_____ 2. Please mail this package for me ____
_____ 3. I love the gift you gave me ____
_____ 4. Lay the papers on the desk ____
_____ 5. How beautiful the night is ____
_____ 6. Watch out for that turning car ____
_____ 7. Drive more slowly ____
_____ 8. Keep time with the music ____
_____ 9. Deliver this message immediately ____
_____ 10. Sign your name in my yearbook ____
_____ 11. That airplane is incredibly huge ____
_____ 12. Please lend me a postage stamp ____
_____ 13. I'm delighted with the flowers ____
_____ 14. How blue the sky is ____
_____ 15. My neighbor's shed is on fire ____
_____ 16. The baby's lip is bleeding ____
_____ 17. I can't believe that I got a perfect score ____
_____ 18. Pass the green beans ____
_____ 19. Write these sentences ____
_____ 20. That movie was very exciting ____
_____ 21. The puppy is extremely playful ____
_____ 22. Look both ways when crossing the street ____
_____ 23. What a pretty red and blue sailboat ____
_____ 24. Please repeat what you said ____
_____ 25. Put the vase on the table ____
_____ 26. Be more careful with your work ____
_____ 27. That's a fantastic book to read ____
_____ 28. This is a wonderful surprise ____

Complete Subjects and Predicates

> - Every sentence has two main parts, a **complete subject** and a **complete predicate.**
> - The complete subject includes all the words that tell who or what the sentence is about.
>   EXAMPLES:
>   **My brother** / likes to go with us.
>   **Six geese** / honked loudly.
> - The complete predicate includes all the words that state the action or condition of the subject.
>   EXAMPLES:
>   My brother / **likes to go with us.**
>   Six geese / **honked loudly.**

 Draw a line between the complete subject and the complete predicate in each sentence.

1. Bees / fly.
2. Trains whistle.
3. A talented artist drew this cartoon.
4. The wind blew furiously.
5. My grandmother made this dress last year.
6. We surely have enjoyed the holiday.
7. These cookies are made with rice.
8. This letter came to the post office box.
9. They rent a cabin in Colorado every summer.
10. Jennifer is reading about the pioneer days in the West.
11. Our baseball team won the third game of the series.
12. The band played a cheerful tune.
13. A cloudless sky is a great help to a pilot.
14. The voice of the auctioneer was heard throughout the hall.
15. A sudden flash of lightning startled us.
16. The wind howled down the chimney.
17. Paul's dog followed him to the grocery store.
18. Their apartment is on the sixth floor.
19. We have studied many interesting places.
20. Each player on the team deserves credit for the victory.
21. Forest rangers fought the raging fire.
22. A friend taught Robert a valuable lesson.
23. Millions of stars make up the Milky Way.
24. The airplane was lost in the thick clouds.
25. Many of the children waded in the pool.
26. Yellowstone Park is a large national park.
27. Cold weather is predicted for tomorrow.
28. The trees were covered with moss.

Name _____ Date _____

Simple Subjects and Predicates

- The **simple subject** of a sentence is the main word in the complete subject.
- The simple subject is a noun or a word that stands for a noun.
    EXAMPLE: My **sister** / lost her gloves.
- Sometimes the simple subject is also the complete subject.
    EXAMPLE: **She** / lost her gloves.
- The **simple predicate** of a sentence is a verb within the complete predicate.
- The simple predicate may be a one-word verb or a verb of more than one word.
    EXAMPLES: She / **lost** her gloves. She / **is looking** for them.

 Draw a line between the complete subject and complete predicate in each sentence below. Underline the simple subject once and the simple predicate twice.

1. A sudden <u>clap</u> of thunder / <u>frightened</u> all of us.
2. The soft snow covered the fields and roads.
3. We drove very slowly over the narrow bridge.
4. The students are making an aquarium.
5. Our class read about the founder of Hull House.
6. The women were talking in the park.
7. This album has many folk songs.
8. We are furnishing the sandwiches for tonight's picnic.
9. All the trees on that lawn are giant oaks.
10. Many Americans are working in foreign countries.
11. The manager read the names of the contest winners.
12. Terrill brought these large melons.
13. We opened the front door of the house.
14. The two mechanics worked on the car for an hour.
15. Black and yellow butterflies fluttered among the flowers.
16. The child spoke politely.
17. We found many beautiful shells along the shore.
18. The best part of the program is the dance number.
19. Every ambitious person is working hard.
20. Sheryl swam across the lake two times.
21. Our program will begin promptly at eight o'clock.
22. The handle of this basket is broken.
23. The clock in the tower strikes every hour.
24. The white farmhouse on that road belongs to my cousin.
25. The first game of the season will be played tomorrow.

Name _____   Date _____

Subjects and Predicates in Inverted Order

- When the subject of a sentence comes before all or part of the predicate, the sentence is in **natural order**.
    - EXAMPLE: The puppy scampered away.
- When all or part of the predicate comes before the subject, the sentence is in **inverted order**.
    - EXAMPLE: Away scampered the puppy.
- Many interrogative sentences are in inverted order.
    - EXAMPLE: Where is / Jamie?

 **Draw a line between the complete subject and the complete predicate in each sentence. Write I in front of sentences that are in inverted order.**

____I____ 1. Lightly falls / the mist.

_____ 2. The peaches on this tree are ripe now.

_____ 3. Over and over rolled the rocks.

_____ 4. Down the street marched the band.

_____ 5. Near the ocean are many birds.

_____ 6. Right under the chair ran the kitten.

_____ 7. He hit the ball a long way.

_____ 8. Along the ridge hiked the campers.

_____ 9. Underground is the stream.

_____ 10. The fish jumped in the lake.

_____ 11. Over the hill came the trucks.

_____ 12. Out came the rainbow.

 Rewrite each of the inverted sentences above in natural order.

13. _____

14. _____

15. _____

16. _____

17. _____

18. _____

19. _____

20. _____

21. _____

Name _____   Date _____

Using Compound Subjects

> - Two sentences in which the subjects are different but the predicates are the same can be combined into one sentence.
> - The two subjects are joined by <u>and</u>.
> - The subject of the new sentence is called a **compound subject**.
>   EXAMPLE:
>   **Lynn** visited an amusement park.
>   **Eric** visited an amusement park.
>   **Lynn** and **Eric** visited an amusement park.

✣ **Draw a line between the complete subject and the complete predicate in each sentence. If the subject is compound, write CS before the sentence.**

__CS__ 1. English settlers and Spanish settlers / came to North America in the 1600s.

_____ 2. Trees and bushes were chopped down to make room for their houses.

_____ 3. The fierce winds and the cold temperatures made the first winters very harsh.

_____ 4. The settlers and Native Americans became friends.

_____ 5. Native Americans helped the settlers grow food in the new country.

_____ 6. Potatoes and corn were first grown by Native Americans.

_____ 7. English settlers and Spanish settlers had never tasted turkey.

_____ 8. Peanuts and sunflower seeds are Native American foods that we now eat for snacks.

_____ 9. Lima beans and corn are combined to make succotash.

_____ 10. Zucchini is an American squash that was renamed by Italian settlers.

_____ 11. Native Americans also introduced barbecuing to the settlers.

✣ **Combine each pair of sentences below. Underline the compound subject.**

12. Gold from the New World was sent to Spain. Silver from the New World was sent to Spain.

_____

_____

13. France staked claims in the Americas in the 1500s and 1600s. The Netherlands staked claims in the Americas in the 1500s and 1600s.

_____

_____

14. John Cabot explored areas of the Americas. Henry Hudson explored areas of the Americas.

_____

_____

 Write a sentence with a compound subject.

15. _____

www.harcourtschoolsupply.com
© Harcourt Achieve Inc. All rights reserved.

Unit 2: Sentences
Language: Usage and Practice 6, SV 1419027832

Name _____ Date _____

Using Compound Predicates

- Two sentences in which the subjects are the same but the predicates are different can be combined into one sentence.
- The two predicates may be joined by <u>or</u>, <u>and</u>, or <u>but</u>.
- The predicate of the new sentence is called a **compound predicate**.
    EXAMPLE:
    The crowd **cheered** the players.
    The crowd **applauded** the players.
    The crowd **cheered** and **applauded** the players.

Draw a line between the complete subject and the complete predicate in each sentence. If the predicate is compound, write <u>CP</u> before the sentence.

_____ 1. The students organized a picnic for their families.

_____ 2. They discussed and chose a date for the picnic.

_____ 3. They wrote and designed invitations.

_____ 4. The invitations were mailed and delivered promptly.

_____ 5. Twenty-five families responded to the invitations.

_____ 6. The students bought the food and made the sandwiches.

_____ 7. The families bought the soft drinks.

_____ 8. The students packed and loaded the food into a truck.

_____ 9. The families brought and set up the volleyball nets.

_____ 10. Everyone participated in the games and races.

_____ 11. They ran relay races and threw water balloons.

_____ 12. Everyone packed the food and cleaned up the picnic area at the end of the day.

Combine each pair of sentences below. Underline the compound predicate.

13. Carrie heard the music. Carrie memorized the music.

_____

_____

14. Keith picked up the newspapers. Keith loaded the newspapers into his car.

_____

_____

15. Lance studied the names of the states. Lance wrote down the names of the states.

_____

_____

Write a sentence with a compound predicate.

16. _____

Name _____   Date _____

Simple and Compound Sentences

- A **simple sentence** has one subject and one predicate.
    EXAMPLE: Earth / is covered by land and water.
- A **compound sentence** is made up of two simple sentences joined by a connecting word such as <u>and</u>, <u>but</u>, and <u>or</u>. A comma is placed before the connecting word.
    EXAMPLE: One fourth of Earth / is covered by land, and the land / is divided into seven continents.

✺ **Draw a line between the complete subject and the complete predicate in each sentence. Write <u>S</u> before each simple sentence. Write <u>C</u> before each compound sentence.**

_____ 1. The seven continents of the world are North America, South America, Africa, Europe, Australia, Asia, and Antarctica.

_____ 2. Three fourths of Earth is covered by water, and most of it is salty ocean water.

_____ 3. The four oceans of the world are the Pacific, the Atlantic, the Indian, and the Arctic.

_____ 4. We cannot exist without water, but we cannot drink the salty ocean water.

_____ 5. Most of the water we drink comes from lakes, rivers, and streams.

_____ 6. Clean water is a priceless resource.

✺ **Combine each pair of simple sentences below into a compound sentence.**

7. The Pacific Ocean is the largest ocean in the world.
   It covers more area than all of Earth's land put together.

   _____
   _____

8. Bodies of salt water that are smaller than oceans are called seas, gulfs, or bays.
   These bodies of water are often encircled by land.

   _____
   _____

9. Seas, gulfs, and bays are joined to the oceans.
   They vary in size and depth.

   _____
   _____

10. The Mediterranean is one of Earth's largest seas.
    It is almost entirely encircled by the southern part of Europe, the northern part of Africa, and the western part of Asia.

    _____
    _____
    _____

Correcting Run-on Sentences

- Two or more sentences run together without the correct punctuation are called a **run-on sentence.**
    EXAMPLE: It will rain today, it will be sunny tomorrow.
- One way to correct a run-on sentence is to separate it into two sentences.
    EXAMPLE: It will rain today. It will be sunny tomorrow.
- Another way to correct a run-on sentence is to separate the two main parts with a comma and <u>and</u>, <u>or</u>, <u>but</u>, <u>nor</u>, or <u>yet</u>.
    EXAMPLE: It will rain today, but it will be sunny tomorrow.

 Rewrite each run-on sentence correctly.

1. In 1860, the Pony Express started in St. Joseph, Missouri, the route began where the railroads ended.

2. People in the West wanted faster mail service, the mail took six weeks by boat.

3. Mail sent by stagecoach took about 21 days, the Pony Express averaged ten days.

4. The Pony Express used a relay system riders and horses were switched at 157 places along the way to Sacramento, California.

5. Because teenagers weighed less than adults, most of the riders were teenagers the horses could run faster carrying them.

6. Riders had to cross raging rivers, the mountains were another barrier.

Name _____ Date _____

Expanding Sentences

> - Sentences can be **expanded** by adding details to make them clearer and more interesting.
>   EXAMPLE: The child waved.
>   The child **in the blue hat** waved **timidly to me**.
> - Details added to sentences may answer these questions: When? (today) Where? (at home) How? (slowly) How often? (daily) To what degree? (very) What kind? (big) Which? (smallest) How many? (five)

Expand each sentence by adding details to answer the questions shown in parentheses. Write the expanded sentence on the line.

1. The ball soared. (What kind? Where?)

   _____

2. It crashed. (How? Where?)

   _____

3. It rolled. (When? Where?)

   _____

4. I felt. (How? To what degree?)

   _____

Decide how each of the following sentences can be expanded. Write your new sentence on the lines.

5. The fires spread. _____

   _____

6. People ran. _____

   _____

7. Homes and trees blazed. _____

   _____

8. Firefighters came. _____

   _____

9. Water sprayed. _____

   _____

10. Flames died out. _____

    _____

Name _____ Date _____

Unit 2 Test

Darken the circle by the phrase that is not a sentence.

1. Ⓐ Here we go!
   Ⓑ Having fun now.
   Ⓒ Let's go eat.
   Ⓓ Will you come?

2. Ⓐ In a minute.
   Ⓑ She was sleeping.
   Ⓒ The storm ended.
   Ⓓ Don't go alone.

3. Ⓐ You should see that!
   Ⓑ Why are you here?
   Ⓒ Do the right thing.
   Ⓓ For my friend.

4. Ⓐ He said nothing.
   Ⓑ It was old.
   Ⓒ Fine for her.
   Ⓓ The dog barked.

Darken the circle by (A) if the group of words is an interrogative sentence, (B) if it is an imperative sentence, (C) if it is an exclamatory sentence, or (D) if it is a declarative sentence.

5. Be careful with that. Ⓐ IN Ⓑ IM Ⓒ E Ⓓ D
6. When did you go? Ⓐ IN Ⓑ IM Ⓒ E Ⓓ D
7. Why did you leave? Ⓐ IN Ⓑ IM Ⓒ E Ⓓ D
8. What a wonderful day it is! Ⓐ IN Ⓑ IM Ⓒ E Ⓓ D
9. I must show her. Ⓐ IN Ⓑ IM Ⓒ E Ⓓ D
10. Don't drop that. Ⓐ IN Ⓑ IM Ⓒ E Ⓓ D
11. Would they come? Ⓐ IN Ⓑ IM Ⓒ E Ⓓ D
12. Be there by noon. Ⓐ IN Ⓑ IM Ⓒ E Ⓓ D
13. He is such a nice person! Ⓐ IN Ⓑ IM Ⓒ E Ⓓ D
14. I'll go down by the river. Ⓐ IN Ⓑ IM Ⓒ E Ⓓ D
15. I was so surprised! Ⓐ IN Ⓑ IM Ⓒ E Ⓓ D
16. What did you say? Ⓐ IN Ⓑ IM Ⓒ E Ⓓ D

Darken the circle by each sentence that has a line drawn between the complete subject and the complete predicate.

17. Ⓐ My sister Claire / likes to swim in the lake before breakfast.
    Ⓑ Sam will / clean the fish that we catch today.
    Ⓒ My brother and sister are / cleaning the sailboat.
    Ⓓ Janice saw / Steven at the lake.

18. Ⓐ The seasons are the / four divisions of the year.
    Ⓑ The origin / of the wheat plant is uncertain.
    Ⓒ Yosemite National Park / is very popular.
    Ⓓ Many towns / in the United States are built near water.

19. Ⓐ I like to study / chemistry and biology.
    Ⓑ My sister / graduated from college last year.
    Ⓒ Many / tourists visit Paris, France, each year.
    Ⓓ The railroad passes through / the middle of the city.

20. Ⓐ My friends and I went to / London last summer.
    Ⓑ The doctor said it's / nothing to worry about.
    Ⓒ I really like the / new computer you bought.
    Ⓓ Pamela / has been sick for three days.

Name _____   Date _____

Unit 2 Test, p. 2

Darken the circle by the sentence in which the simple subject is underlined.

21. Ⓐ They caught all <u>kinds</u> of fish.
    Ⓑ <u>My dog</u> has fleas.
    Ⓒ <u>This</u> is my favorite tool.
    Ⓓ <u>Her</u> only brother is visiting.

22. Ⓐ The warm <u>climate</u> attracts visitors.
    Ⓑ The people <u>boarded</u> a train.
    Ⓒ The tall <u>pine</u> trees hid the cabin.
    Ⓓ She filled the <u>vase</u> with flowers.

Darken the circle by the sentence in which the simple predicate is underlined.

23. Ⓐ <u>Jerry closed</u> the store early.
    Ⓑ Karen <u>has been</u> on vacation.
    Ⓒ Jacob <u>can</u> play the flute.
    Ⓓ We <u>saw them</u> yesterday.

24. Ⓐ She <u>spoke politely</u>.
    Ⓑ The first game will <u>be</u> tomorrow.
    Ⓒ Our program <u>is starting</u> soon.
    Ⓓ The handle <u>broke in</u> half.

Darken the circle by the sentence that is in inverted order.

25. Ⓐ Down came the rain.
    Ⓑ She fell on the ice.
    Ⓒ The cat scratched the chair.
    Ⓓ The judge is coming.

26. Ⓐ Tell me about it.
    Ⓑ How did that happen?
    Ⓒ We went up the stairs.
    Ⓓ The dish fell and broke.

Darken the circle by the sentence that has a compound subject.

27. Ⓐ Teo went fishing and hiking.
    Ⓑ The boys waded out into the stream.
    Ⓒ Carla and Cassie cooked dinner.
    Ⓓ The storm howled and raged.

Darken the circle by the sentence that has a compound predicate.

28. Ⓐ She made and wrapped all her presents.
    Ⓑ The clerk added up the numbers.
    Ⓒ He turned around slowly.
    Ⓓ Forty men and women attended.

Darken the circle by the sentence that is a compound sentence.

29. Ⓐ I would like to go, but I can't.
    Ⓑ Last night we saw Alex and Sara at the movie theater.
    Ⓒ Jenna and Elena will help Zack wash the car tomorrow.
    Ⓓ Would you like fish or chicken for lunch, Ladonna?

30. Ⓐ Yes, I prefer to go home.
    Ⓑ She wanted to go to the first game of the season.
    Ⓒ You can go with him, or you can stay with me.
    Ⓓ Since when do you like to watch football?

Darken the circle by the sentence that is a run-on sentence.

31. Ⓐ My grandfather works as a janitor at a hospital.
    Ⓑ He enjoys working with his hands, and he likes to meet new people.
    Ⓒ He once fixed our furnace, it's worked well ever since.
    Ⓓ My mom says that I got my common sense from Grandpa.

32. Ⓐ Have you ever seen the Statue of Liberty, it's in New York?
    Ⓑ The statue is copper, and it was given to the United States by France in 1884.
    Ⓒ The statue's official name is *Liberty Enlightening the World*.
    Ⓓ Each year approximately two million people visit the Statue of Liberty.

Name _____   Date _____

Nouns

> • A **noun** is a word that names a person, place, thing, or quality.
> EXAMPLES: boy, Maria, river, Wyoming, house, beach, joy

Write nouns that name the following:

1. Four famous people

2. Four types of jobs

3. Four places you would like to visit

4. Four vegetables

5. Four qualities you would like to possess

Underline each noun.

6. Alaska is rich in gold, silver, copper, and oil.
7. Chocolate is made from the beans of a tree that grows in the tropics.
8. The distance across Texas is greater than the distance from Chicago to New York.
9. The men and women rode their horses in the parade.
10. The oldest city in California is San Diego.
11. Alexander Graham Bell, the inventor of the telephone, was born in Edinburgh, Scotland.
12. Jack, Diane, and I took a plane to London, where we saw Buckingham Palace.
13. Many interesting animals, such as piranhas, alligators, anacondas, and sloths, live in the Amazon River Basin.
14. The tarantula is a type of large, hairy spider.
15. The Maya were a people who lived in what is now Mexico and Central America.

Name _____ Date _____

Common and Proper Nouns

- There are two main types of nouns: **common nouns** and **proper nouns**.
- A **common noun** names any one of a class of objects.
    EXAMPLES: girl   state   author
- A **proper noun** is the name of a particular person, place, or thing. A proper noun begins with a capital letter.
    EXAMPLES: Mark Twain   Tennessee   Washington Monument

 Write a proper noun suggested by each common noun.

1. college _____
2. river _____
3. governor _____
4. singer _____
5. physician _____
6. holiday _____
7. TV show _____
8. city _____
9. teacher _____
10. classmate _____
11. car _____
12. school _____
13. lake _____
14. country _____
15. street _____
16. park _____
17. month _____
18. actor _____
19. girl _____
20. state _____

 Write a common noun suggested by each proper noun.

21. Rhode Island _____
22. South America _____
23. Tuesday _____
24. Nile _____
25. Dr. Washington _____
26. Lake Erie _____
27. Thanksgiving _____
28. Pacific _____
29. Alabama _____
30. Daniel _____
31. Mars _____
32. J. D. Rowling _____
33. February _____
34. Andes Mountains _____
35. Mexico _____
36. *Treasure Island* _____
37. Jennifer _____
38. London _____
39. Washington, D.C. _____
40. Fido _____

Common and Proper Nouns, p. 2

 Underline each common noun.

41. The sturdy timber of the oak is used in constructing furniture, bridges, and ships.
42. Robert Fulton was a painter, jeweler, farmer, engineer, and inventor.
43. The main crops of Puerto Rico are sugar, tobacco, coffee, and fruits.
44. The pecan groves of Texas provide nuts for the eastern part of the United States.
45. France has many rivers and beaches.
46. The Verrazano-Narrows Bridge between Brooklyn and Staten Island is the longest suspension bridge in the world.
47. Some of the main foods eaten in Greece are lamb, fish, olives, and feta cheese.
48. A road passes through a tunnel cut in the base of a giant tree in California.
49. Since the earliest civilizations, gold has been used for ornaments.
50. One of the largest lakes in North America is Lake Erie.
51. The orange tree bears beautiful blossoms and delicious fruits.
52. Rockefeller Center is a large business and entertainment center in New York.
53. Pine trees give us turpentine, tar, resin, timber, and oils.
54. The United States buys the greatest amount of the world's coffee.
55. The pelican, the penguin, and the flamingo are interesting birds.
56. The first trip into space was filled with danger.

 Underline each proper noun.

57. The principal goods exported by Brazil are soybeans, sugar, and coffee.
58. William Penn was the founder of Pennsylvania.
59. On the shelves of the Elm Grove Library, you will find many magical stories.
60. Commander Byrd, a naval officer, made the first airplane flight to the North Pole.
61. Dr. Jeanne Spurlock went to Howard University College of Medicine.
62. The orange tree was brought to Europe from Asia.
63. Colombia is a leading producer of emeralds.
64. Kilimanjaro is the tallest mountain in Africa.
65. The Navajo make beautiful silver and turquoise jewelry.
66. Bena and Carlos anchored the tent while Sam and Teri prepared the food.
67. Thomas Jefferson introduced the decimal system of coinage (dollars, dimes, cents) that is now used in the United States.
68. Their home is on the shore of Lake Michigan.
69. Quebec is the only city in North America that has a wall around it.
70. Paul Revere was a patriot, a silversmith, an engraver, and a dentist.
71. Lemons were first grown in the valleys of India.
72. The Sears Tower in Chicago is a tall building.

Name _____   Date _____

Singular and Plural Nouns

- A **singular noun** names one person, place, or thing.
  EXAMPLES: girl, half, pear, sky
- A **plural noun** names more than one person, place, or thing.
  EXAMPLES: girls, halves, pears, skies
- Add s to most nouns to make them plural.
  EXAMPLES: girl, girls   top, tops
- Add es to most nouns ending in ch, sh, s, or x to make them plural.
  EXAMPLES: church, churches   brush, brushes   ax, axes
- If a noun ends in a consonant and y, change the y to i and add es.
  EXAMPLES: city, cities   army, armies
- If a noun ends in a vowel and y, add s to make it plural.
  EXAMPLE: boy, boys

 Write the plural form for each noun below.

1. newspaper _____
2. guess _____
3. town _____
4. valley _____
5. body _____
6. story _____
7. bush _____
8. office _____

9. tax _____
10. toy _____
11. boss _____
12. school _____
13. day _____
14. copy _____
15. author _____
16. porch _____

 Complete each sentence with the plural form of the noun in parentheses.

17. (penny)   How many _____ make a dollar?

18. (dress)   Marcy makes all of her own _____.

19. (bridge) How many _____ were destroyed by the flood?

20. (brush)   Mr. Perez got two new _____ yesterday.

21. (county) How many _____ are there in your state?

22. (fox)   Seven _____ live at the zoo.

23. (book)   I like to read _____ about our pioneers.

24. (lunch)   She made several _____ before school.

25. (country) How many _____ are there in South America?

Name _____ Date _____

Singular and Plural Nouns, p. 2

- Some nouns ending in f or fe are made plural by changing the f or fe to ves.
    EXAMPLES: loaf, loaves   wife, wives
- Some nouns ending in f are made plural by adding s.
    EXAMPLES: roof, roofs   bluff, bluffs
- Most nouns ending in o that have a vowel just before the o are made plural by adding s.
    EXAMPLE: radio, radios
- Some nouns ending in o preceded by a consonant are made plural by adding es, but others are made plural by adding only s.
    EXAMPLES: potato, potatoes   piano, pianos
- A few nouns have irregular plural forms.
    EXAMPLES: child, children   man, men   ox, oxen
- A few nouns have the same form for both the singular and plural.
    EXAMPLES: trout, trout   sheep, sheep

 Write the plural form for each noun below. You might wish to check the spellings in a dictionary.

26. knife _____

27. loaf _____

28. half _____

29. mouse _____

30. foot _____

31. goose _____

32. hoof _____

33. moose _____

34. life _____

35. tomato _____

36. tooth _____

37. piano _____

 Complete each sentence with the plural form of the word in parentheses. You may wish to check the spellings in a dictionary.

38. (foot)   My new shoes pinch my _____.

39. (sheep)   The shepherd always takes good care of the _____.

40. (chimney)   Many _____ were blown down during the recent storm.

41. (city)   Many _____ are establishing recreation centers.

42. (leaf)   The high winds scattered the dead _____ over the yard.

43. (Mosquito)   _____ breed wherever there is standing water.

44. (nickel)   I have five Jefferson _____.

45. (friend)   Her _____ arrived on the bus yesterday.

46. (desk)   New _____ have been ordered for our office.

47. (bench)   Concrete _____ have been placed along the walk.

Name _____ Date _____

Possessive Nouns

- A **possessive noun** shows possession of the noun that follows.
- Form the possessive of most singular nouns by adding an apostrophe (') and s.
    EXAMPLES: the boy's hat   Mr. Thomas's car
- Form the possessive of a plural noun ending in s by adding only an apostrophe.
    EXAMPLES: the Smiths' home   girls' bikes   sisters' names
- Form the possessive of a plural noun that does not end in s by adding an apostrophe and s.
    EXAMPLES: children's classes   men's books

Write the possessive form of each noun.

1. girl _____
2. child _____
3. women _____
4. children _____
5. John _____
6. baby _____
7. boys _____
8. teacher _____
9. Dr. Ray _____
10. ladies _____
11. brother _____
12. soldier _____
13. men _____
14. aunt _____
15. Ms. Jones _____

Rewrite each phrase using a possessive noun.

16. the cap belonging to Jim _____
17. the wrench that belongs to Kathy _____
18. the smile of the baby _____
19. the car that my friend owns _____
20. the new shoes that belong to Kim _____
21. the collar of the dog _____
22. the golf clubs that Frank owns _____
23. the shoes that belong to the runners _____
24. the friends of our parents _____
25. the opinion of the editor _____
26. the lunches of the children _____
27. the coat belonging to Kyle _____
28. the assignment of the teacher _____

Name _____   Date _____

Possessive Nouns, p. 2

Complete each sentence with the possessive form of the word in parentheses.

29. (company)   The _____ picnic will be at the park Saturday afternoon.

30. (dog)   That _____ owner should pay for the damage it did.

31. (women)   The _____ organization planned the meeting.

32. (Doug)   _____ account of his trip was very interesting.

33. (David)   _____ explanation of the problem was very clear.

34. (cat)   My _____ eyes are blue.

35. (Kurt)   _____ brother made the candy for our party.

36. (Men)   _____ coats are sold at the store in that block.

37. (squirrel)   The _____ teeth were very sharp.

38. (brother)   We want to go to his _____ ranch.

39. (child)   A _____ toy was found in our yard.

40. (calf)   The _____ nose was soft and shiny.

41. (baby)   That dog played with the _____ shoe.

42. (teachers)   Her _____ names are Miss Gomez and Mr. Jacobs.

43. (Alex)   We are going to _____ party tomorrow.

44. (deer)   They saw a _____ tracks in the snow.

45. (Stacy)   _____ work is the neatest I have ever seen.

46. (country)   We display our _____ flag every day.

47. (robins)   I have heard those _____ calls every day this week.

48. (person)   That _____ speech was much too long.

49. (sister)   Nichole wants to go to her _____ graduation.

50. (children)   The _____ parade is held every spring.

51. (neighbors)   Our _____ yards have just been mowed.

52. (class)   It is this _____ time to take the test.

53. (boys)   This store sells _____ clothes.

54. (designer)   The _____ exhibit won first place.

55. (horse)   The _____ mane is black.

www.harcourtschoolsupply.com   Unit 3: Grammar and Usage
© Harcourt Achieve Inc. All rights reserved.   Language: Usage and Practice 6, SV 1419027832

Name _____ Date _____

Appositives

> - An **appositive** is a noun or phrase that identifies or explains the noun it follows.
> - Use a comma before and after an appositive. If an appositive is at the end of a sentence, use a comma before it.
>   EXAMPLES:
>   Jenna is graduating from Spring Hill, her **junior high school.**
>   Christopher's baseball team, **the Padres**, won every game they played.

 Circle the appositive in each sentence. Underline the noun it identifies or explains.

1. Henry, my father's older brother, drove trains.
2. His train, the Missouri Pacific, carried mostly freight.
3. Seattle, the location of the main station, was where the freight was loaded.
4. Coal and lumber, its main cargo, was then shipped east.
5. When Henry, our uncle, came to visit, we asked many questions.
6. He never tired of telling us, his nephews, about his life.
7. Uncle Henry would joke with my father, his brother, and they laughed a great deal.
8. Uncle Henry would tease my mother, his sister-in-law, too.
9. We especially liked it when he brought Aunt Emma, his wife, with him.
10. It was nice to see our cousins, Todd and Elizabeth, too.

 Write sentences using the appositives below.

11. the cleanest room in the house   _Our living room, the cleanest room in the house, is usually kept for entertaining company._

12. the most interesting subject _____

13. the best day of the week _____

14. my favorite sport _____

15. a movie star _____

16. a tropical island _____

Verbs

> - A **verb** is a word that expresses action, being, or state of being.
>   EXAMPLES: Christine **went** to school.
>   These books **are** yours.
>   Liza and Paul **sing** in the choir.

 Underline the verb in each sentence.

1. Where are the Alps?
2. W. C. Handy wrote "Saint Louis Blues."
3. Check your papers carefully.
4. Bananas have great food value.
5. Africa is the home of the hippopotamus.
6. The car reached the narrow bridge.
7. Gwendolyn Brooks won a Pulitzer Prize.
8. Elizabeth's father trains good mechanics.
9. Suzi has a black puppy.
10. How many stars are on the United States flag?
11. The people of our town remember the cold winter.
12. Peter Minuit bought Manhattan Island for about twenty-four dollars.
13. What is your favorite book?
14. They followed the old trail to the top of the hill.
15. The wind whistled around the corner.
16. Eric always watches the news.
17. Their team scored twice in the third quarter.
18. Which driver won the auto race?
19. The third house from the corner is white.
20. Mexico lies to the south of the United States.
21. Tom set the table for five people.
22. Answer my question.
23. Lucy explained the operation of the computer.
24. Jason worked in the flower bed for his neighbor.
25. Our town has a public swimming pool.
26. My brother plays the saxophone.
27. Brush your teeth frequently.
28. A puff of wind whirled the leaves over the lawn.
29. We arrived at our camp early in the morning.
30. Where is the launching pad?

Name _____ Date _____

Verb Phrases

- Some sentences contain a **verb phrase**.
- A verb phrase consists of a **main verb** and one or more other verbs.
  EXAMPLES: The women **are singing**.
  Where **have** you **been**?

 Underline the verb or verb phrase in each sentence.

1. The first American schools were held in homes.
2. Who invented the jet engine?
3. *The New England Primer* was the earliest United States textbook.
4. John Philip Sousa was a bandmaster and composer.
5. Who built the first motorcycle?
6. My friends will arrive on Saturday afternoon.
7. What was the final score?
8. Ryan has made this unusual birdhouse.
9. The waves covered the beach with many shells.
10. I have ridden on a motor scooter.
11. The artist is molding clay.
12. Britney and her friends spent last summer in the mountains.
13. The names of the new employees are posted by the supervisor.
14. Pablo has found a new hat.
15. She is going to the store.
16. We have trimmed the hedges.
17. The United States exports many kinds of food.
18. My friend is reading a book about World War I.
19. Jane Addams helped many foreign-born people in Chicago, Illinois.
20. Oil was discovered in many parts of North America.
21. Jenny Lind was called the Swedish Nightingale.
22. We are planning a car trip to Miami, Florida.
23. That dog has howled for two hours.
24. Our guests have arrived.
25. I have written letters to several companies.
26. I can name two important cities in that country.
27. The hummingbird received its name because of the sound of its wings.
28. Jon's poem was printed in the newspaper.
29. Charles and Akeem are working at the hamburger stand.
30. This table was painted recently.

Helping Verbs

- The last word of a verb phrase is the main verb. The other words are **helping verbs.**

    EXAMPLES: helping verb   main verb

    Bella and Jon **were** sitting on the bench.
    Many apples **are** displayed by the produce manager.

- The helping verbs are:
    am, are, is, was, were, be, being, been
    has, have, had
    do, does, did
    can, could, must, may, might, shall, should, will, would

 Underline the verb phrase and circle the helping verb in each sentence below.

1. We (have) begun our spring cleaning.
2. Mike and Anne will rake the leaves on the front lawn.
3. Vincent and April must sweep the driveway.
4. The twins, Dawn and Daniela, will pull the weeds.
5. Christopher and his cousin, Lena, may prepare lunch for the workers.
6. They should wash their hands first.
7. Sandwiches and fruit salad would make a delicious lunch on a hot day.
8. Our next-door neighbor is working on his lawn, too.
9. He has sprayed his front and back lawns with a fertilizer.
10. Every helper must close the garbage bags tightly.
11. Squirrels, raccoons, and large crows would enjoy our garbage.
12. We might finish the outside work today.

 Use each verb phrase in a sentence.

13. would come _____
14. should choose _____
15. had bought _____
16. might find _____
17. am writing _____
18. will learn _____
19. could become _____
20. were standing _____

Name _____ Date _____

More Helping Verbs

> - A verb phrase may have more than one helping verb.
>   EXAMPLES: **helping verb**   **main verb**
>
>   Bart   **should have**   **taken** the bus.
>   My plants **have been**   **growing** very quickly.
> - In a question or a sentence containing a word such as <u>not</u> or <u>never</u>, the helping verb might be separated from the main verb.
>   EXAMPLES:
>   When **will** you **decide** to fix your bicycle?
>   Jason **has** not **fixed** his bicycle.

 Underline the verb phrases and circle the helping verbs in the sentences below.

1. Our final exam (will be) given on May 10.
2. Many students have been studying every night.
3. My friends and I may be forming a study group.
4. The study group members should be reviewing each chapter.
5. Are you joining our study group?
6. May we meet in your house one afternoon next week?
7. Kim and Tim should have known the answers to the first ten questions.
8. Where have you been all day?
9. I have been looking everywhere for you.
10. I would have met you earlier.
11. The airplane flight has been delayed in Chicago.
12. Would you prefer an earlier flight?
13. No, I had been enjoying a long visit with my grandmother.
14. My parents have been waiting for over two hours in the airport.
15. Lois and Jean had been at the pool all day.
16. Will any other friends be swimming in the pool?
17. Several neighborhood children must have been splashing each other.
18. Could Jessica and I take diving lessons next summer?

 Use each verb phrase in a statement.

19. should have bought _____

20. had been finished _____

 Use each verb phrase in a question.

21. will be going _____

22. have been practicing _____

Name _____ Date _____

Using *Is/Are* and *Was/Were*

- Use is with a singular subject.
    EXAMPLE: Tasha **is** the winner.
- Use are with a plural subject.
    EXAMPLE: The boys **are** walking home.
- Always use are with the pronoun you.
    EXAMPLE: You **are** absolutely right!

 Underline the correct verb to complete each sentence.

1. (Is, Are) this tool ready to be cleaned?
2. They (is, are) making peanut brittle.
3. LaRoy (is, are) the chairperson this week.
4. Where (is, are) my gloves?
5. This tomato (is, are) too ripe.
6. Rianne, (is, are) these your books?
7. Daniel, (is, are) the sandwiches ready?
8. (Is, Are) you going to sing your solo this morning?
9. This newspaper (is, are) the early edition.
10. Chen asked if you (is, are) still coming to the game.

- Use was with a singular subject to tell about the past.
    EXAMPLE: I **was** there yesterday.
- Use were with a plural subject to tell about the past.
    EXAMPLE: Roy and Ray **were** not home.
- Always use were with the pronoun you.
    EXAMPLE: You **were** only a few minutes late.

 Underline the correct verb to complete each sentence.

11. Amy and Crystal (was, were) disappointed because they could not go.
12. Our seats (was, were) near the stage.
13. Taro, Bill, and Luis (was, were) assigned to the first team.
14. These pencils (was, were) made by a company in Atlanta.
15. There (was, were) only one carton of milk in the refrigerator.
16. Who (was, were) that person on the corner?
17. She (was, were) at my house this morning.
18. You (was, were) the best swimmer in the contest.
19. Those tomatoes (was, were) delicious!
20. He (was, were) late for work today.

Name _____ Date _____

Verb Tenses

- The **tense** of a verb tells the time of the action or being.
- **Present tense** tells that something is happening now.
  EXAMPLES:
  Amanda **dances** in the show.
  My art lessons **start** today.
- **Past tense** tells that something happened in the past. The action is over.
  EXAMPLES:
  Amanda **danced** in the show.
  My art lessons **started** last June.
- **Future tense** tells that something will happen in the future. Use <u>will</u> with the verb.
  EXAMPLES:
  Amanda **will dance** in the show.
  My art lessons **will start** next month.

 Underline the verb or verb phrase in each sentence. Then write <u>present</u>, <u>past</u>, or <u>future</u> to tell the tense of each verb.

1. My neighbor works four days a week. _____
2. Sometimes I care for her children, Kara and Willy. _____
3. They play in front of my house. _____
4. One day Kara threw the ball very hard to Willy. _____
5. The ball sailed over Willy's head and into the street. _____
6. Willy ran toward the street. _____
7. I shouted to Willy. _____
8. Usually, Willy listens to me. _____
9. I got the ball from the street. _____
10. Willy's mom called for him to come home. _____
11. He went as fast as possible. _____
12. Next time they will play only in the backyard. _____

Rewrite each sentence, changing the underlined verb to the past tense.

13. My little sister <u>will follow</u> me everywhere.

    _____

14. She <u>comes</u> to my friend's house.

    _____

15. She <u>rides</u> my bicycle on the grass.

    _____

Name _____ Date _____

Principal Parts of Verbs

- A verb has four principal parts: **present, present participle, past,** and **past participle.**
- For **regular verbs,** the present participle is formed by adding <u>ing</u> to the present. It is used with a form of the helping verb <u>be</u>.
- The past and past participles are formed by adding <u>ed</u> to the present. The past participle uses a form of the helping verb <u>have</u>.

    EXAMPLES:

Present	Present Participle	Past	Past Participle
walk	(is) walking	walked	(have, has, had) walked
point	(is) pointing	pointed	(have, has, had) pointed
cook	(is) cooking	cooked	(have, has, had) cooked

- **Irregular verbs** form their past and past participles in other ways. A dictionary shows the principal parts of these verbs.

 Write the present participle, past, and past participle for each verb.

PRESENT	PRESENT PARTICIPLE	PAST	PAST PARTICIPLE
1. walk	_____	_____	_____
2. visit	_____	_____	_____
3. watch	_____	_____	_____
4. follow	_____	_____	_____
5. jump	_____	_____	_____
6. talk	_____	_____	_____
7. add	_____	_____	_____
8. learn	_____	_____	_____
9. paint	_____	_____	_____
10. plant	_____	_____	_____
11. work	_____	_____	_____
12. divide	_____	_____	_____
13. miss	_____	_____	_____
14. score	_____	_____	_____
15. call	_____	_____	_____
16. collect	_____	_____	_____

Past Tenses of *See*, *Do*, and *Come*

- Never use a helping verb with saw, did, or came.
- Always use a helping verb with seen, done, and come.

 Underline the correct verb form to complete each sentence.

1. We (saw, seen) the movie.
2. Suddenly, the whole idea (came, come) to me.
3. Tara and Jon (did, done) not do the ironing this morning.
4. They (saw, seen) that a lot of work had to be done to the camp.
5. Who (did, done) the framing of these prints?
6. The rain (came, come) down in sheets.
7. I haven't (did, done) all the errands for Anna.
8. I have (came, come) to help arrange the stage.
9. We have (saw, seen) many miles of beautiful prairie flowers.
10. What have you (did, done) with the kittens?
11. My uncle (came, come) to help me move.
12. I have not (saw, seen) the new apartment today.
13. Why haven't your brothers (came, come) to help us?
14. Haven't you ever (saw, seen) a spider spinning a web?
15. When Tonya and I (came, come) in, we found a surprise.
16. I (saw, seen) the owner about the job.
17. We saw what you (did, done)!
18. Has the mail (came, come) yet?
19. The prettiest place we (saw, seen) was the Grand Canyon.
20. Hasn't Kyle (did, done) a nice job of painting the room?
21. Mr. Jones (came, come) to repair the stove.
22. My dog, Max, (did, done) that trick twice.
23. Josh hadn't (came, come) to the soccer game.
24. Rebecca (saw, seen) the doctor yesterday.
25. Scott has (came, come) to the picnic.
26. Who has (saw, seen) the Rocky Mountains?
27. Delia (did, done) the decorations for the party.
28. She (came, come) to the party an hour early.
29. The bird (saw, seen) the cat near the tree.
30. The painter has (did, done) a nice job on the house.

Name _____ Date _____

Past Tenses of *Eat* and *Drink*

- Never use a helping verb with ate or drank.
- Always use a helping verb with eaten and drunk.

Underline the correct verb form to complete each sentence.

1. Have the worms (ate, eaten) the leaves on that tree?
2. We (drank, drunk) the spring water from the mountains.
3. You (ate, eaten) more for breakfast than I did.
4. Haven't you (drank, drunk) a glass of this refreshing lemonade?
5. The hungry hikers (ate, eaten) quickly.
6. Yes, I (drank, drunk) two glasses of lemonade.
7. Have you (ate, eaten) your lunch so soon?
8. Marie, why haven't you (drank, drunk) your tea?
9. I (ate, eaten) two delicious hamburgers for lunch.
10. We watched the birds as they (drank, drunk) from the birdbath.
11. We (ate, eaten) supper early.
12. Who (drank, drunk) a glass of tomato juice?
13. Have you ever (ate, eaten) a pink grapefruit?
14. Leeza, have you (drank, drunk) an extra glass of milk?
15. Have you (ate, eaten) your breakfast yet?
16. Yes, I (drank, drunk) it about noon.

Write the correct past tense form of each verb in parentheses to complete each sentence.

17. (eat)   Marci had _____ turkey and stuffing at Thanksgiving.
18. (drink) She _____ cranberry juice for breakfast.
19. (eat)   Carlos _____ a second sandwich.
20. (drink) At the picnic we had _____ a gallon of lemonade.
21. (drink) Yes, I _____ a glass of lemonade.
22. (eat)   Cory hasn't _____ since breakfast.
23. (drink) Father _____ a glass of iced tea.
24. (eat)   Did you know that those apples had been _____?
25. (drink) Haven't Mike and Lisa _____ the fresh orange juice?
26. (eat)   The people on the train _____ in the dining car.

Name _____ Date _____

Past Tenses of *Sing* and *Ring*

- Never use a helping verb with sang or rang.
- Always use a helping verb with sung and rung.

 Underline the correct verb form to complete each sentence.

1. I have never (sang, sung) in public before.
2. Have the church bells (rang, rung)?
3. The group (sang, sung) all their college songs for us.
4. The bell had not (rang, rung) at five o'clock.
5. The children (sang, sung) three patriotic songs.
6. We (rang, rung) their doorbell several times.
7. Which of the three sisters (sang, sung) in the talent show?
8. Who (rang, rung) the outside bell?
9. Patti, have you ever (sang, sung) for the choir director?
10. I (rang, rung) the old bell that is beside the door.
11. Has she ever (sang, sung) this duet?
12. The Liberty Bell hasn't (rang, rung) in many years.
13. The group (sang, sung) as they had never (sang, sung) before.
14. The ship's bell hasn't (rang, rung).
15. The Canadian singer often (sang, sung) that song.
16. Have you (rang, rung) the bell on that post?

Write the correct past tense form of the verb in parentheses to complete each sentence.

17. (ring) It was so noisy that we couldn't tell if the bell had _____.
18. (sing) Kayla _____ a solo.
19. (sing) She had never _____ alone before.
20. (ring) The bells _____ to announce their marriage yesterday.
21. (ring) Have you _____ the bell yet?
22. (sing) Who _____ the first song?
23. (ring) The group _____ bells to play a tune.
24. (sing) Hasn't she _____ before royalty?
25. (ring) The boxer jumped up as the bell _____.
26. (sing) That young boy _____ a solo.

Name _____   Date _____

Past Tenses of *Freeze, Choose, Speak,* and *Break*

- Never use a helping verb with froze, chose, spoke, or broke.
- Always use a helping verb with frozen, chosen, spoken, and broken.

 Underline the correct verb form to complete each sentence.

1. Haven't those candidates (spoke, spoken) yet?
2. Has the dessert (froze, frozen) in the molds?
3. I (broke, broken) the handle of the hammer.
4. Have you (spoke, spoken) to your friends about the meeting?
5. Hadn't the coach (chose, chosen) the best players today?
6. The dog has (broke, broken) the toy.
7. Has Angie (spoke, spoken) to you about going with us?
8. We (froze, frozen) the ice for our picnic.
9. I believe you (chose, chosen) the right clothes.
10. Jarret, haven't you (broke, broken) your bat?
11. Mr. Mann (spoke, spoken) first.
12. Antonio (froze, frozen) the fruit salad for our picnic.
13. You didn't tell me he had (broke, broken) his arm.
14. The men on the team (chose, chosen) their plays carefully.
15. Ms. Ramirez (spoke, spoken) first.
16. Has the river (froze, frozen) yet?

 Write the correct past tense form of the verb in parentheses to complete each sentence.

17. (freeze) We could not tell if the ice had _____ overnight.
18. (break) The chain on Han's bicycle had _____ while he rode.
19. (choose) Carla had _____ to be in the play.
20. (speak) No one _____ while the band played.
21. (choose) Ava has _____ to take both tests today.
22. (choose) Jim _____ not to take the test early.
23. (break) No one knew who had _____ the window.
24. (speak) Brigid _____ her lines loudly and clearly.
25. (freeze) It was so cold that everything had _____.
26. (speak) The librarian wanted to know who had _____ so loudly.

Name _____ Date _____

Past Tenses of *Know, Grow,* and *Throw*

- Never use a helping verb with knew, grew, or threw.
- Always use a helping verb with known, grown, and thrown.

Underline the correct verb form to complete each sentence.

1. We have (knew, known) her family for years.
2. Weeds (grew, grown) along the park paths.
3. Hasn't Julia (threw, thrown) the softball?
4. I have never (knew, known) a more courageous person.
5. Katy's plants have (grew, grown) very rapidly.
6. How many times have you (threw, thrown) at the target?
7. Has Jackson (grew, grown) any unusual plants this year?
8. I (knew, known) every person at the meeting.
9. I wish that my hair hadn't (grew, grown) so much this year.
10. Brianne, how long have you (knew, known) Lee?
11. The pitcher has (threw, thrown) three strikes in a row.
12. I don't know why the plants (grew, grown) so fast.
13. We (threw, thrown) out many old boxes.
14. Mr. Lo has (grew, grown) vegetables this summer.
15. Marley (knew, known) the correct answer.
16. The guard (threw, thrown) the ball to the center.
17. She is the nicest person I have ever (knew, known).
18. The sun (grew, grown) brighter in the afternoon.

Write one sentence with knew. Then write one sentence with known.

19. _____
20. _____

Write one sentence with grew. Then write one sentence with grown.

21. _____
22. _____

Write one sentence with threw. Then write one sentence with thrown.

23. _____
24. _____

Name _____   Date _____

Past Tenses of *Blow* and *Fly*

- Never use a helping verb with blew or flew.
- Always use a helping verb with blown and flown.

 Underline the correct verb form to complete each sentence.

1. Flags (flew, flown) from many houses on the Fourth of July.
2. The train whistles have (blew, blown) at every crossing.
3. The birds haven't (flew, flown) south for the winter.
4. The wind (blew, blown) the kites to pieces.
5. The candles (blew, blown) out too soon.
6. Has your friend (flew, flown) her new kite?
7. Yes, she (flew, flown) it this morning.
8. All the papers have (blew, blown) across the floor.
9. Four people (flew, flown) their model airplanes in the tournament.
10. The wind has (blew, blown) like this for an hour.
11. I didn't know that you had (flew, flown) here in a jet.
12. Hasn't the train whistle (blew, blown) yet?
13. The airplanes (flew, flown) in an aviation show.
14. Our largest maple tree had (blew, blown) down last night.
15. The striped hot-air balloon has (flew, flown) the farthest.
16. The judge (blew, blown) the whistle as the runner crossed the finish line.
17. The Carsons have (flew, flown) to Europe.
18. An erupting volcano (blew, blown) the mountain apart.
19. The geese (flew, flown) in formation.
20. The curtains have (blew, blown) open from the breeze.
21. The movie star (flew, flown) in a private jet.
22. A tornado (blew, blown) the roof off a house.
23. A pair of ducks has (flew, flown) overhead.

 Write one sentence with blew. Then write one sentence with blown.

24. _____
25. _____

 Write one sentence with flew. Then write one sentence with flown.

26. _____
27. _____

Name _____   Date _____

Past Tenses of *Take* and *Write*

- Never use a helping verb with <u>took</u> or <u>wrote</u>.
- Always use a helping verb with <u>taken</u> and <u>written</u>.

Underline the correct verb form to complete each sentence.

1. They (took, taken) the first plane to Tampa.
2. Who has (wrote, written) the best script for the play?
3. Mitchell hadn't (took, taken) these pictures last summer.
4. Who (wrote, written) the minutes of our last meeting?
5. We (took, taken) down our paintings.
6. Marguerite Henry has (wrote, written) many stories about horses.
7. I (took, taken) my watch to the jeweler for repair.
8. I (wrote, written) for a video catalog.
9. Haven't you (took, taken) your medicine yet?
10. Diana, have you (wrote, written) to your friend?
11. Pedro (took, taken) too much time getting ready.
12. Ladeena hadn't (wrote, written) these exercises with a pen.
13. Who (took, taken) my magazine?
14. Mario (wrote, written) an excellent business letter.

Write the correct past tense form of the verb in parentheses to complete each sentence.

15. (write)   Who _____ this short theme?
16. (take)   It has _____ me a long time to make this planter.
17. (write)   Eve Merriam had _____ this poem.
18. (take)   The children have _____ off their muddy shoes.
19. (write)   We _____ letters to our state senators.
20. (take)   Reya, have you _____ your dog for a walk?
21. (write)   My cousin _____ me a letter about his new house.
22. (write)   Robert Frost _____ David's favorite poem.
23. (take)   Willie and Sharona _____ the bus to the park.
24. (write)   Mr. Bustos _____ an excellent article for our newspaper.
25. (take)   The nurse _____ my temperature.

Name _____ Date _____

Past Tenses of *Give* and *Go*

- Never use a helping verb with gave or went.
- Always use a helping verb with given and gone.

Underline the correct verb form to complete each sentence.

1. Ms. Morris has (gave, given) that land to the city.
2. Where has Darla (went, gone) this afternoon?
3. Carlos (gave, given) a speech on collecting rare coins.
4. My friends (went, gone) to the park an hour ago.
5. Kary, who (gave, given) you this ruby ring?
6. Rob and Carter have (went, gone) to paint the house.
7. Mr. White (gave, given) us ten minutes to take the test.
8. Elaine has (went, gone) to help Haley find the place.
9. My friends (gave, given) clothing to the people whose house burned.
10. Hasn't Jenny (went, gone) to the store yet?
11. The sportscaster has just (gave, given) the latest baseball scores.
12. Chuck (went, gone) to apply for the job.
13. Have you (gave, given) Fluffy her food?
14. Has Miss Martinson (went, gone) to Springfield?
15. I have (gave, given) my horn to my cousin.
16. Paulina has (went, gone) to sleep already.

Write the correct past tense form of the verb in parentheses to complete each sentence.

17. (go)   Ming _____ to sleep already.
18. (give) Has Mrs. Tate _____ the checks to the other employees?
19. (go)   Every person had _____ before you arrived.
20. (give) My neighbor was _____ a ticket for speeding.
21. (go)   Haven't the Yamadas _____ to Japan for a month?
22. (give) Ms. O'Malley has _____ me a notebook.
23. (go)   Haven't you ever _____ to an aquarium?
24. (give) I _____ her my new address.
25. (go)   Michael _____ to camp for a week.
26. (give) Ms. Rosen has _____ me driving lessons.

Unit 3: Grammar and Usage

Name _____ Date _____

Possessive Pronouns

- A **possessive pronoun** is a pronoun that shows ownership of something.
- The possessive pronouns hers, mine, ours, theirs, and yours stand alone.
    EXAMPLES: The coat is **mine**. The shoes are **yours**.
- The possessive pronouns her, its, my, our, their, and your must be used before nouns.
    EXAMPLES: **Her** car is red. **Our** car is black.
- The pronoun his may be used either way.
    EXAMPLES: That is **his** dog. The dog is **his**.

 Underline the possessive pronoun in each sentence.

1. Lora lost her bracelet.
2. Brady broke his arm.
3. The dogs wagged their tails.
4. The referee blew her whistle.
5. The students should take their books.
6. Musician Louis Armstrong was famous for his smile.
7. Brad entered his sculpture in the contest.
8. I wanted to read that book, but a number of its pages are missing.
9. My aunt and uncle have sold their Arizona ranch.
10. The Inuit build their igloos out of snow blocks.
11. How did Florida get its name?
12. Jake showed the group his wonderful stamp collection.
13. Coffee found its way from Arabia to Java.
14. The magpie builds its nest very carefully.
15. Allison sprained her ankle while skiing.
16. Lisa drove her car to the top of the peak.
17. Frank left his raincoat in the doctor's office.
18. Isn't Alaska noted for its salmon?
19. Travis brought his mother a beautiful shawl from India.
20. Gina, where is your brother?
21. Manuel forgot about his appointment with the dentist.
22. Nick and Andrew have gone to their swimming lesson.
23. Sandra showed her report to the boss.
24. Juan gave his father a beautiful paperweight.
25. Mr. Owens found his keys.
26. The children broke their swing.

Name _____ Date _____

Indefinite Pronouns

- An **indefinite pronoun** is a pronoun that does not refer to a specific person or thing.
  - EXAMPLES: **Someone** is coming to speak to the group.
  - Does **anyone** know what time it is?
  - **Everybody** is looking forward to the trip.
- Some indefinite pronouns are negative.
  - EXAMPLES: **Nobody** has a ticket.
  - **No one** was waiting at the bus stop.
- The indefinite pronouns anybody, anyone, anything, each, everyone, everybody, everything, nobody, no one, nothing, somebody, someone, and something are singular. They take singular verbs.
  - EXAMPLE: **Everyone is** ready.
- The indefinite pronouns both, few, many, several, and some are plural. They take plural verbs.
  - EXAMPLE: **Several** of us **are** ready.

 Underline the indefinite pronoun in each sentence below.

1. Everyone helped complete the project.
2. Is somebody waiting for you?
3. Anything is possible.
4. Something arrived in the mail.
5. Everybody looked tired at practice.
6. No one was willing to work longer.
7. Does anyone have a dollar?
8. Both of us were tired.
9. Nothing was dry yet.
10. Does anybody want to go swimming?
11. Someone should speak up.
12. Everybody is hungry now.
13. Each of the cats was black.
14. Some of the dogs bark all the time.
15. Several were empty.
16. No one remembered to bring it.
17. Everyone started to feel nervous.
18. Nobody admitted to being afraid.
19. Everything will be explained.
20. Is anything missing?

 Complete each sentence with an indefinite pronoun.

21. I can't believe that _____ in my desk disappeared.
22. Is _____ coming to teach you to run the computer?
23. Every person in class attended today. _____ was absent.
24. She tried to call, but _____ answered the phone.
25. Does _____ remember the address?
26. There is _____ here to see you.
27. Would _____ like a piece of cake?
28. The party was so much fun. _____ enjoyed it.

Name _____ Date _____

Subject Pronouns

- A **subject pronoun** is used as the subject or as part of the subject of a sentence.
- The subject pronouns are I, you, he, she, it, we, and they.
    EXAMPLE: **It** has beautiful wings.
- When the pronoun I is used with nouns or other pronouns, it is always named last.
    EXAMPLE: Tyler and **I** caught a butterfly.

 Underline the correct pronoun to complete each sentence.

1. Justin and (I, me) helped repair the car.
2. (She, Her) is going to the studio.
3. Why can't Leigh and (I, me) go with them?
4. (She, Her) and Charles skated all afternoon.
5. Jaclyn and (I, me) are going to Chicago tomorrow.
6. (He, Him) played tennis this morning.
7. Sameera and (he, him) were five minutes late yesterday morning.
8. (She, Her) and (I, me) spent an hour in the library.
9. Norton and (I, me) worked until nine o'clock.
10. (He, Him) and Yuri are going over there now.
11. May (we, us) carry your packages?
12. (They, Them) and I are buying some groceries.
13. Ravi and (I, me) are going with her to the park.
14. (It, Them) wagged its tail.
15. (She, You) have a beautiful singing voice, Claire.
16. (He, Him) is the owner of the suitcase.
17. Crystal and (I, me) are on the same team.
18. (She, Her) has started a book club.
19. (We, Us) are planning a bike trip.
20. (They, Them) are going to see a Shakespearean play.
21. Is (she, her) your favorite singer?
22. Martin and (I, me) would be happy to help you.
23. (We, Us) work at the post office.
24. Juan and (we, us) are painting the front porch.
25. (He, Him) excels as a photographer.
26. (She, Her) has known us for several years.
27. (I, Me) am the director of the community choir.

Name _____   Date _____

Object Pronouns

- An **object pronoun** is used after an action verb or a preposition such as <u>after</u>, <u>against</u>, <u>at</u>, <u>between</u>, <u>except</u>, <u>for</u>, <u>from</u>, <u>in</u>, <u>of</u>, <u>to</u>, and <u>with</u>.
- The object pronouns are <u>me</u>, <u>you</u>, <u>him</u>, <u>her</u>, <u>it</u>, <u>us</u>, and <u>them</u>.
    EXAMPLE: The gift was for **him**.
- When the pronoun <u>me</u> is used with nouns or other pronouns, it is always last.
    EXAMPLE: The books were for Kay and **me**.

 Underline the correct pronoun to complete each sentence.

1. Tony, are you going with Yolani and (I, me) to see Rosa?
2. Scott invited Patrick and (I, me) to a movie.
3. I am going to see Mary and (she, her) about this problem.
4. The woman told (us, we) to come for her old magazines.
5. I went with Jan and (she, her) to the hobby show.
6. That dinner was prepared by (them, they).
7. Jim asked Rick and (I, me) to the soccer game.
8. Emily and Latoya congratulated (he, him).
9. Sharon praised (him, he) for his work.
10. Will you talk to (she, her) about the trip?
11. Ben, can you go with Renee and (I, me)?
12. Johnna lectured (us, we) about being on time.
13. The package was addressed to (us, we).
14. They brought the problem to (we, us).
15. It was too hard for (they, them) to solve.
16. Leo gave (I, me) his old goalie's equipment.
17. Derrick is teaching (we, us) Morse code.
18. Please inform (he, him) of the change of plans.
19. Brian offered to help (I, me) hang the curtains.
20. That car belongs to (he, him).
21. Carl didn't see (they, them).
22. Teena asked him to take a picture of (we, us).
23. Please wait for (she, her) after school.
24. She is in the class with (he, him).
25. Hand the package to (they, them).
26. Was this really discovered by (she, her)?
27. Would you like to go to dinner with (we, us)?

Name _____ Date _____

Subject Pronouns After Linking Verbs

- A linking verb connects the subject of a sentence with a noun or adjective that comes after the linking verb.

  EXAMPLES: **Subject**   **Linking Verb**   **Noun**

  The **baby**   was   Christopher.

  The **baseball players**   were   my friends.

- Use a subject pronoun after a linking verb.

  EXAMPLES: The **baby**   was   he.

  The **baseball players**   were   they.

- Use a subject pronoun after such phrases as it is or it was.

  EXAMPLE: It was I who asked the question.

 Underline the correct pronoun to complete each sentence.

1. It was (I, me) who found the keys.
2. It was (she, her) who lost them.
3. The detectives were (we, us).
4. It was (they, them) who looked in the mailbox.
5. The letter carrier is (she, her).
6. It was (he, him) on the telephone.
7. The speakers were Jerald and (I, me).
8. The athlete was (she, her).
9. The photographer was (he, him).
10. That young woman is (she, her).
11. The helper is (he, him).
12. My partners are (they, them).
13. Was it (he, him) who told you?
14. The winner of the race is (she, her).
15. It was (we, us) who were chosen.
16. Was it (I, me) who made the error?

 Complete these sentences by writing a subject pronoun for the word or words in parentheses.

17. It was _____ who worked out in the gym.   (the basketball team)

18. The most talented gymnast is _____.   (Shannon)

19. Our newest team members are _____.   (Jason and Mark)

20. The coach with the whistle is _____.   (Lauren)

21. The spectators in the gym were _____.   (my friends)

22. The one who is on the parallel bars is _____.   (Kurt)

23. The one who is on the balance beam is _____.   (Kristin)

24. Our best vaulter is _____.   (Michelle)

25. The athlete on the rings was _____.   (Bill)

26. The vice president of the company is _____.   (Ms. Walker)

Name _____ Date _____

Using *Who/Whom*

- Use who as a subject pronoun.
    EXAMPLE: **Who** came to the party?
- Use whom as an object pronoun.
    EXAMPLE: **Whom** did the nurse help?
- By rearranging the sentence The nurse did help **whom**?, you can see that whom follows the verb and is the object of the verb. It can also be the object of a preposition.
    EXAMPLE: To **whom** did you wish to speak?

 Complete each sentence with Who or Whom.

1. _____ is that man?
2. _____ made the first moon landing?
3. _____ would you choose as the winner?
4. _____ is your best friend?
5. _____ gets the reward?
6. _____ will be staying with you this summer?
7. _____ did the instructor invite to speak to the class?
8. _____ did you see at the park?
9. _____ will you contact at headquarters?
10. _____ will you write about?
11. _____ is available to babysit for me on Saturday?
12. _____ did you drive to the store?
13. _____ would like to travel to Hawaii next summer?
14. _____ raced in the track meet?
15. _____ did they meet at the airport?
16. _____ are your three favorite authors?
17. _____ owns the new blue car?
18. _____ did you help last week?
19. _____ wrote that clever poem?
20. _____ will you ask to help you move?
21. _____ brought that salad?

Using Pronouns

 Underline the pronouns in each sentence below.

1. He went with us to the picnic by the lake.
2. Did you find a magazine in the living room?
3. When are we going to meet at the concert?
4. Are we leaving today?
5. Did you see him?
6. She saw them at the party.
7. He spoke to Chip and me.
8. Who brought the music for you to play?
9. Kristin and I invited them to go to a movie.
10. Marsha brought me these pictures she took.
11. Why can't they go with us?
12. I went with her to get the application form.
13. Louis brought you and him some French coins.
14. Between you and me, I think that last program was silly.
15. Did Dottie explain the experiment to her and him?
16. Did she find them?
17. May I go with you?
18. He and I sat on the benches.
19. They saw me this morning.
20. Who has a library book?
21. For whom shall I ask?
22. I do not have it with me.
23. She told me about the trip to Canada.
24. They are coming to see us.
25. We haven't heard from Brittan since he left.
26. Come with us.
27. Aren't you and I going with Alana?
28. You should plan the theme before you write it.
29. Aren't they coming for us?
30. Kelly and I gave them a new book of stamps.
31. Steve told us an interesting story about a dog.
32. Who is planning a summer vacation?
33. She and I never expected to see you here!
34. We will visit them this evening.

Name _____ Date _____

More Pronouns

 Underline the correct pronoun to complete each sentence.

1. It was (I, me).
2. William and (he, him) are on their way to catch the plane.
3. Nicole and (I, me) have always been good friends.
4. The guard showed (they, them) the entrance to the building.
5. The boss told (I, me) to clean the office.
6. Please take (I, me) to lunch.
7. I am going to wait for (she, her).
8. (Who, Whom) planted those beautiful flowers?
9. Next Saturday Nick and (I, me) are going fishing.
10. Marcie came to see (us, we).
11. To (who, whom) did you send the postcard?
12. This is a secret between you and (I, me).
13. Hector told Carolyn to move (us, our) table.
14. The committee asked Michael, Kip, and (I, me) to help serve.
15. Did Latricia bring (she, her)?
16. Jacey told (us, we) to get to the station on time.
17. Grant and (she, her) drove the tractors.
18. (Who, Whom) bought this magazine?
19. The boss brought Matt and Morgan (them, their) checks.
20. Martin took Armando and (I, me) to work this morning.
21. With (who, whom) did you play soccer?
22. Michelle painted (she, her) kitchen yesterday.
23. Seven of (us, we) were named to the board of directors.
24. He completed all of (his, him) math problems this morning.
25. (Us, We) are going to play basketball.
26. She called for Janice and (I, me).
27. (Who, Whom) washed the windows?
28. Kim and (I, me) will fix the broken latch.
29. We came to see (them, they).
30. Will Pamela or (I, me) go with Jason to (him, his) ranch?
31. For (who, whom) are you looking?
32. Did you know it was (her, she)?
33. Lisa and (her, she) are painting the chairs.
34. (We, Us) are going to the museum on Saturday.

Name _____ Date _____

Adjectives

- An **adjective** is a word that describes a noun or a pronoun.
    EXAMPLE: The sky is dotted with **fluffy** clouds.
- Adjectives usually tell what kind, which one, or how many.
    EXAMPLES: **yellow** roses   **that** mitt   **sixty** cents

 Choose an appropriate adjective from the box to describe each noun.

| brave | foolish | gorgeous | hasty | shiny |
| cold | fragrant | happy | polite | sly |

1. _____ scout
2. _____ flower
3. _____ worker
4. _____ water
5. _____ fox

6. _____ girls
7. _____ sunset
8. _____ dimes
9. _____ prank
10. _____ deeds

 Write three adjectives that could be used to describe each noun.

11. flowers _____ _____ _____
12. an automobile _____ _____ _____
13. a friend _____ _____ _____
14. a bicycle _____ _____ _____
15. snow _____ _____ _____
16. a baby _____ _____ _____
17. a sunrise _____ _____ _____
18. a book _____ _____ _____
19. a kitten _____ _____ _____
20. a train _____ _____ _____
21. a mountain _____ _____ _____
22. the wind _____ _____ _____
23. a river _____ _____ _____
24. a house _____ _____ _____

Name _____   Date _____

Articles

- The **articles** a, an, and the are called **limiting adjectives**.
- Use a before words beginning with a consonant sound.
  EXAMPLES: **a** bugle   **a** mountain   **a** snail
- Use an before words beginning with a vowel sound.
  EXAMPLES: **an** oboe   **an** island   **an** anchor

 Write a or an to describe each noun.

1. _____ salesperson
2. _____ train
3. _____ newspaper
4. _____ iceberg
5. _____ friend
6. _____ election
7. _____ welder
8. _____ piano
9. _____ game
10. _____ ant
11. _____ eye
12. _____ army
13. _____ telephone
14. _____ orange
15. _____ country
16. _____ airplane
17. _____ oak
18. _____ engine
19. _____ ear
20. _____ state
21. _____ elm
22. _____ shoe
23. _____ object
24. _____ basket
25. _____ apple

26. _____ ounce
27. _____ error
28. _____ tablet
29. _____ desk
30. _____ holiday
31. _____ accident
32. _____ astronaut
33. _____ box
34. _____ fire
35. _____ pilot
36. _____ mechanic
37. _____ entrance
38. _____ evergreen
39. _____ aviator
40. _____ hundred
41. _____ picture
42. _____ elephant
43. _____ letter
44. _____ umbrella
45. _____ announcer
46. _____ onion
47. _____ umpire
48. _____ car
49. _____ ice cube
50. _____ elevator

Name _____ Date _____

Proper Adjectives

> - A **proper adjective** is an adjective that is formed from a proper noun.
> - It always begins with a capital letter.
>   EXAMPLES:
> | Proper Noun | Proper Adjective |
> |---|---|
> | Poland | Polish |
> | Germany | German |
> | Paris | Parisian |

 Write a proper adjective formed from each proper noun below. You may wish to check the spelling in a dictionary.

1. South America _____
2. Africa _____
3. England _____
4. Mexico _____
5. France _____
6. Russia _____
7. America _____
8. Rome _____
9. Alaska _____
10. Canada _____
11. Norway _____
12. Scotland _____
13. Ireland _____
14. China _____
15. Spain _____
16. Italy _____
17. Hawaii _____
18. Japan _____

 Write sentences using proper adjectives you formed above.

19. _____ Many South American countries have warm climates. _____
20. _____
21. _____
22. _____
23. _____
24. _____
25. _____
26. _____
27. _____
28. _____

Name _____   Date _____

Demonstrative Adjectives

- A **demonstrative adjective** is an adjective that points out a specific person or thing.
- <u>This</u> and <u>that</u> describe singular nouns. <u>This</u> points to a person or thing nearby, and <u>that</u> points to a person or thing farther away.
    EXAMPLES:
        This room is my favorite.
        That man is running very fast.
- <u>These</u> and <u>those</u> describe plural nouns. <u>These</u> points to persons or things nearby, and <u>those</u> points to persons or things farther away.
    EXAMPLES:
        These women are the best players.
        Those houses need painting.
- The word <u>them</u> is a pronoun. Never use it to describe a noun.

 Underline the correct demonstrative adjective to complete each sentence.

1. Please hand me (those, this) red candles.
2. Where did you buy (these, that) large pecans?
3. Did you grow (these, them) roses in your garden?
4. Please bring me (those, that) wrench.
5. Where did Marc find (these, this) watermelon?
6. (Those, Them) glasses belong to Mike.
7. Do you want one of (these, this) calendars?
8. May I use one of (these, them) pencils?
9. Did you see (those, them) films about Africa?
10. Calvin, where are (those, that) people going?
11. Did you see (those, them) police officers?
12. Please put (those, this) books in the box.
13. (That, those) floor needs to be cleaned.
14. Sari and Josh might buy (those, that) car.
15. (That, These) cabinets will be repainted.
16. Please close (that, those) door.
17. Will you fix the flat tire on (this, these) bike?
18. (This, Those) letter needs a stamp before you mail it.

 Write four sentences using <u>this</u>, <u>that</u>, <u>these</u>, or <u>those</u>.

19. _____
20. _____
21. _____
22. _____

Name _____ Date _____

Comparing with Adjectives

- An adjective has three degrees of comparison: **positive, comparative,** and **superlative**.
- The simple form of the adjective is called the positive **degree.**
  - EXAMPLE: Anita is **tall.**
- When two people or things are being compared, the **comparative degree** is used.
  - EXAMPLE: Anita is **taller** than Natalie.
- When three or more people or things are being compared, the **superlative degree** is used.
  - EXAMPLE: Anita is the **tallest** person in the group.
- For all adjectives of one syllable and a few adjectives of two syllables, add <u>er</u> to form the comparative degree and <u>est</u> to form the superlative degree.
  - EXAMPLE: rich   richer   richest
- If the adjective ends in <u>y</u>, change the <u>y</u> to <u>i</u> and add <u>er</u> or <u>est</u>.
  - EXAMPLE: tiny   tinier   tiniest

 Write the comparative and superlative forms.

POSITIVE	COMPARATIVE	SUPERLATIVE
1. smooth		
2. young		
3. sweet		
4. strong		
5. lazy		
6. great		
7. kind		
8. calm		
9. rough		
10. narrow		
11. deep		
12. short		
13. happy		
14. cold		
15. pretty		

Name _____ Date _____

More Comparing with Adjectives

- For some adjectives of two syllables and all adjectives of three or more syllables, use more to form the comparative and most to form the superlative.
   EXAMPLES:
   He thinks that the lily is **more** fragrant than the tulip.
   He thinks that the carnation is the **most** fragrant flower of all.
- Comparison of adjectives also can be used to indicate less or least of a quality. Use less to form the comparative and least to form the superlative.
   EXAMPLES:
   I see Terry **less** often than I see Tony.
   I see Josh **least** often of all.
- Some adjectives have irregular comparisons.
   EXAMPLES: good, better, best   bad, worse, worst

Write the comparative and superlative forms using more and most.

POSITIVE	COMPARATIVE	SUPERLATIVE
1. energetic	_____	_____
2. courteous	_____	_____
3. impatient	_____	_____
4. important	_____	_____
5. difficult	_____	_____
6. wonderful	_____	_____
7. gracious	_____	_____
8. agreeable	_____	_____

Write the comparative and superlative forms using less and least.

POSITIVE	COMPARATIVE	SUPERLATIVE
9. helpful	_____	_____
10. friendly	_____	_____
11. serious	_____	_____
12. agreeable	_____	_____
13. faithful	_____	_____
14. comfortable	_____	_____
15. patient	_____	_____
16. reliable	_____	_____

Unit 3: Grammar and Usage
Language: Usage and Practice 6, SV 1419027832

Name _____   Date _____

More Comparing with Adjectives, p. 2

❋ **Write the correct degree of comparison for the adjective in parentheses.**

17. (near)   Which planet is _____ Earth, Venus or Jupiter?

18. (tall)   Who is the _____ of the three people?

19. (helpful)   Who is _____, Sandra or Rebekah?

20. (young)   Who is _____, Mick or Mack?

21. (difficult)   I think this is the _____ problem in the lesson.

22. (good)   Is "A Ghost Story" a _____ story than "The Last Leaf"?

23. (small)   What is our _____ state?

24. (hot)   In our region, August is usually the _____ month.

25. (young)   Hans is the _____ person at the factory.

26. (wide)   The Amazon is the _____ river in the world.

27. (old)   Who is _____, Andy or Steve?

28. (large)   What is the _____ city in your state?

29. (courteous)   Dan is always the _____ person at a party.

30. (good)   This poem is the _____ one I have read this year.

31. (cold)   This must be the _____ night so far this winter.

32. (studious)   Of the two sisters, Andrea is the _____.

33. (tall)   Who is _____, Kay or Jay?

34. (wealthy)   This is the home of the _____ banker in our city.

35. (fast)   Who is the _____ worker in the office?

36. (useful)   Which is _____, electric lights or the telephone?

37. (beautiful)   Your garden is the _____ one I have seen.

38. (narrow)   That is the _____ of all the bridges on the road.

39. (large)   Cleveland is _____ than Cincinnati.

40. (good)   Of the three books, this one is the _____.

41. (bad)   That is the _____ collection in the museum.

42. (famous)   Washington became the _____ general of the Revolution.

43. (beautiful)   I think tulips are the _____ kind of flower.

Name _____ Date _____

Adverbs

- An **adverb** is a word that describes a verb, an adjective, or another adverb.
  EXAMPLES: The parade moved **slowly**.
  Your tie is **very** colorful.
  You did this too **quickly**.
- An adverb usually tells how, when, where, or how often.
- Many adverbs end in <u>ly</u>.

 Write two adverbs that could be used to describe each verb.

1. laugh _____
2. talk _____
3. stand _____
4. sing _____
5. swim _____
6. eat _____

7. read _____
8. work _____
9. write _____
10. walk _____
11. jump _____
12. move _____

13. run _____
14. speak _____
15. listen _____
16. drive _____
17. sit _____
18. dance _____

 Use each adverb in a sentence.

| well | regularly | early |
| softly | very | here |

19. _____
20. _____
21. _____
22. _____
23. _____
24. _____

Adverbs, p. 2

 Underline the adverb or adverbs in each sentence.

25. The old car moved slowly up the hill.
26. She answered him very quickly.
27. We arrived at the party too early, so we helped with the decorations.
28. The family waited patiently to hear about the newborn baby.
29. Cindi drove the car very cautiously in the snowstorm.
30. Does Marshall always sit here, or may I have this seat?
31. They walked very rapidly in order to get home before the rainstorm.
32. The dog ran swiftly toward its home.
33. Emma quietly waited her turn while others went ahead.
34. These oaks grow very slowly, but they are worth the long wait.
35. May I speak now, or should I wait for his call?
36. We searched everywhere for the inflatable rafts and life preservers.
37. The nights have been extremely warm, so we go swimming every evening.
38. He always speaks distinctly and practices good manners.
39. Can you swim far underwater without coming up for air?
40. Come here, and I'll show you ladybugs in the grass.
41. Please answer quickly so that we can finish before five o'clock.
42. Deer run very fast, especially at the first sign of danger.
43. I suddenly remembered that I left my jacket in the park.
44. The snow fell softly on the rooftops of the mountain village.
45. I can pack our lunches and be there by noon.
46. She wrote too rapidly and made a mistake.
47. Winters there are extremely cold, but summers are very pleasant.
48. The pianist bowed politely to the audience.
49. You are reading too rapidly to learn something from it.
50. The team played extremely well.
51. The cat walked softly toward a fly on the windowpane.
52. Everyone listened carefully to the sound of a bluebird singing.
53. We walked wearily toward the bus in the hot sun.
54. We crossed the street very carefully at the beginning of the parade.
55. We eagerly watched the game from the rooftop deck of our building.
56. The recreation center was finished recently.
57. We walked everywhere yesterday.
58. My friend dearly loves her red hat.
59. I have read this book before.
60. He wants badly to learn to play the guitar.

Name _____ Date _____

Comparing with Adverbs

- An adverb has three degrees of comparison: positive, comparative, and superlative.
- The simple form of the adverb is called the **positive degree.**
    EXAMPLE: Joe worked **hard** to complete the job.
- When two actions are being compared, the **comparative degree** is used.
    EXAMPLE: Joe worked **harder** than Jim.
- When three or more actions are being compared, the **superlative degree** is used.
    EXAMPLE: Tony worked **hardest** of all.
- Use er to form the comparative degree and use est to form the superlative degree of one-syllable adverbs.
- Use more or most with longer adverbs and with adverbs that end in ly.
    EXAMPLE: Jan danced **more** gracefully than Tania. Vicki danced the **most** gracefully of all.

Complete each sentence using the comparative or superlative form of the underlined adverb.

1. David can jump high. Diane can jump _____ than David.

    Donna can jump the _____ of all.

2. Grant arrives late for the party. Gina arrives _____ than Grant.

    Gail arrives the _____ of anyone.

3. Dawn walks slowly in the park. Leron walks _____ than Dawn.

    Samuel walks the _____ of all.

4. Jasper spoke clearly before the class. Jon spoke _____ than Jasper.

    Joseph spoke the _____ of all the students.

5. Alex scrubbed hard. Anne scrubbed _____ than Alex.

    Alicia scrubbed the _____ of all.

6. You can lose weight quickly by running. A nutritious diet works _____

    than just running. Of all weight-loss programs, combining the two works the

    _____ .

7. Tania played the flute beautifully. Tara played the clarinet even _____ .

    Rick played the oboe the _____ of them all.

8. Chris has been waiting long. Mr. Norris has been waiting even _____ .

    Justin has been waiting the _____ of all.

www.harcourtschoolsupply.com
© Harcourt Achieve Inc. All rights reserved.

Unit 3: Grammar and Usage
Language: Usage and Practice 6, SV 1419027832

Name _____   Date _____

Using *Doesn't* and *Don't*

- **Doesn't** is the contraction of <u>does not</u>. Use it with singular nouns and the pronouns <u>he</u>, <u>she</u>, and <u>it</u>.
    EXAMPLES:
    The dog **doesn't** want to play.
    She **doesn't** want to go.
- **Don't** is the contraction of <u>do not</u>. Use it with plural nouns and the pronouns <u>I</u>, <u>you</u>, <u>we</u>, and <u>they</u>.
    EXAMPLES:
    The children **don't** have their books.
    We **don't** have time.

 Underline the correct contraction to complete each sentence.

1. I (doesn't, don't) know why he (doesn't, don't) like that movie star.
2. Why (doesn't, don't) the caretaker open the gates earlier?
3. (Doesn't, Don't) your sister coach the team, Todd?
4. (Doesn't, Don't) this office need more fresh air?
5. (Doesn't, Don't) this sweater belong to you, Katie?
6. We (doesn't, don't) go home at noon for lunch.
7. (Doesn't, Don't) your friend attend the state university?
8. Ashley (doesn't, don't) want to miss the parade.
9. Angelo (doesn't, don't) like to play tennis.
10. It (doesn't, don't) take long to learn to swim.
11. Some of the elevators (doesn't, don't) go to the top floor.
12. Eric (doesn't, don't) know how to drive a car.
13. He (doesn't, don't) know that we are here.
14. We (doesn't, don't) listen to our radio often.
15. Why (doesn't, don't) Jeff get here on time?
16. This problem (doesn't, don't) seem difficult to me.
17. (Doesn't, Don't) it look hot outside?
18. Why (doesn't, don't) Paulie go, too?
19. She (doesn't, don't) want to go to the movie.
20. Kelly (doesn't, don't) have that written in her notebook.
21. (Doesn't, Don't) you want to go with us?
22. Why (doesn't, don't) your friend come to our meetings?
23. Neil (doesn't, don't) go to night school.
24. Melissa (doesn't, don't) eat ice cream.
25. Jody and Ray (doesn't, don't) like science-fiction movies.
26. The people (doesn't, don't) have to wait outside.
27. (Doesn't, Don't) you want to come with us?
28. They (doesn't, don't) know if it will rain today.

Name _____ Date _____

Using *May/Can* and *Teach/Learn*

> - Use <u>may</u> to ask for permission.
>   EXAMPLE: **May** I go with you?
> - Use <u>can</u> to express the ability to do something.
>   EXAMPLE: Jason **can** swim well.

 Complete each sentence correctly with <u>may</u> or <u>can</u>.

1. Adam, _____ you whistle?

2. His dog _____ do three difficult tricks.

3. Miss Nance, _____ I leave work early?

4. I _____ see the airplane in the distance.

5. Chris, _____ you tie a good knot?

6. Carlos, _____ I drive your car?

7. You _____ see the mountains from here.

8. My friend _____ drive us home.

9. The Garcias _____ speak three languages.

10. _____ I examine those new books?

> - <u>Teach</u> means "to give instruction."
>   EXAMPLE: I'll **teach** you how to throw a football.
> - <u>Learn</u> means "to acquire knowledge."
>   EXAMPLE: When did you **learn** to speak French?

 Complete each sentence correctly with <u>teach</u> or <u>learn</u>.

11. I think he will _____ me quickly.

12. I will _____ to recite that poem.

13. Did Aaron _____ you to build a fire?

14. The women are going to _____ to use the new machines.

15. Will you _____ me to play tennis?

16. My brother is going to _____ Jillian to skate.

17. Would you like to _____ the rules of the game to them?

18. No one can _____ you if you do not try to _____.

Name _____ Date _____

Using *Sit/Set* and *Lie/Lay*

- Sit means "to take a resting position." Its principal parts are sit, sitting, and sat.
  EXAMPLES:
  Please **sit** here.
  He **sat** beside her.
- Set means "to place." Its principal parts are set, setting, and set.
  EXAMPLES:
  Will you please **set** this dish on the table?
  She **set** the table for dinner last night.

 Underline the correct verb in parentheses to complete each sentence.

1. Please (sit, set) down, Kathleen.
2. Where should we (sit, set) the television?
3. Where do you (sit, set)?
4. Pamela, please (sit, set) those plants out this afternoon.
5. (Sit, Set) the basket of groceries on the patio.
6. Don usually (sits, sets) on this side of the table.
7. Please come and (sit, set) your books on that desk.
8. Have you ever (sat, set) by this window?
9. Does he (sit, set) in this seat?
10. Why don't you (sit, set) over here?

- Lie means "to recline" or "to occupy a certain space." Its principal parts are lie, lying, lay, and lain.
  EXAMPLES:
  Why don't you **lie** down for a while?
  He has **lain** in the hammock all afternoon.
- Lay means "to place." Its principal parts are lay, laying, and laid.
  EXAMPLES:
  The men are **laying** new carpet in the house.
  Who **laid** the wet towel on the table?

 Underline the correct verb in parentheses to complete each sentence.

11. Where did you (lie, lay) your gloves, Dad?
12. (Lie, Lay) down, Spot.
13. He always (lies, lays) down to rest when he is very tired.
14. Where have you (lain, laid) the evening paper?
15. Please (lie, lay) this box on the desk.
16. Do not (lie, lay) on that dusty hay.
17. (Lay, Lie) the papers on top of the desk.
18. I (laid, lain) the shovel on that pile of dirt.
19. I need to (lie, lay) down to rest.
20. She has (laid, lain) on the sofa all morning.

Prepositions

- A **preposition** is a word that shows the relationship of a noun or a pronoun to another word in the sentence.
  EXAMPLES:
  Put the package **on** the table.
  Place the package **in** the desk.
- These are some commonly used prepositions:

about	against	at	between	from	of	through	under
above	among	behind	by	in	on	to	upon
across	around	beside	for	into	over	toward	with

 Draw a line under the preposition or prepositions in the sentences below.

1. The grin on Juan's face was bright and warm.
2. He greeted his cousin from Brazil with a smile and a handshake.
3. They walked through the airport and toward the baggage area.
4. Juan found his bags between two boxes.
5. The two cousins had not seen each other for five years.
6. They could spend hours talking about everything.
7. Juan and Luis got into Juan's truck.
8. Juan drove Luis to Juan's family's ranch.
9. It was a long ride across many hills and fields.
10. Luis rested his head against the seat.
11. Soon they drove over a hill and into a valley.
12. The ranch was located across the Harrison River.
13. The house stood among a group of oak trees.
14. Juan parked the truck beside the driveway.
15. They walked across the driveway and toward the house.
16. Juan's mother, Anita, stood behind the screen door.
17. Juan's family gathered around Luis.
18. Everyone sat on the porch and drank lemonade.
19. "Tell us about our relatives in Brazil," Rosa requested.
20. "You have more than twenty cousins in my area," said Luis.
21. "They go to school, just as you do."
22. Then everyone went into the house and ate dinner.
23. Juan's family passed the food across the table.
24. "Many of these dishes come from old family recipes," he said.
25. "It is wonderful to be among so many relatives," Luis said.
26. After dinner, everyone went to the living room.
27. Luis showed them photographs of his home in Brazil.

Name _____ Date _____

Prepositional Phrases

- A **prepositional phrase** is a group of words that begins with a preposition and ends with a noun or pronoun.
    EXAMPLE: Count the books **on the shelf.**
- The noun or pronoun in a prepositional phrase is called the **object of the preposition.**
    EXAMPLE: Count the books on the **shelf.**

 Put parentheses around each prepositional phrase. Then underline each preposition and circle the object of the preposition.

1. The founders of the United States had a vision of a great country.
2. We climbed into the station wagon.
3. Many stars can be seen on a clear night.
4. The top of my desk has been varnished.
5. Have you ever gone through a tunnel?
6. Place these memos on the bulletin board.
7. We have a display of posters in the showcase in the corridor.
8. Carline, take these reports to Ms. Garza.
9. What is the capital of Alabama?
10. The fabric on this antique sofa came from France.
11. Are you a collector of minerals?
12. I am going to Julia's house.
13. The hillside was dotted with beautiful wildflowers.
14. The rain beat against the windowpanes.
15. We placed a horseshoe above the door.
16. This poem was written by my oldest sister.
17. Great clusters of grapes hung from the vine.
18. Is he going to the race?
19. A herd of goats grazed on the hillside.
20. Are you carrying those books to the storeroom?
21. Our car stalled on the bridge.
22. My family lives in St. Louis.
23. A small vase of flowers was placed in the center of the table.
24. The group sat around the fireplace.
25. The cold wind blew from the north.
26. Dori hit the ball over the fence.
27. The dog played with the bone.
28. High weeds grow by the narrow path.

Name _____ Date _____

Prepositional Phrases as Adjectives/Adverbs

- A prepositional phrase can be used to describe a noun or a pronoun.
- Then the prepositional phrase is being used as an adjective to tell which one, what kind, or how many.
    - EXAMPLE: The chair **in the corner** needs to be repaired.
    - The prepositional phrase in the corner tells which chair.
- A prepositional phrase can be used to describe a verb.
- Then the prepositional phrase is being used as an adverb to tell how, where, or when.
    - EXAMPLE: Mrs. Porter repaired the chair **during the evening.**
    - The prepositional phrase during the evening tells when Mrs. Porter repaired the chair.

 Underline the prepositional phrase in each sentence. Write adjective or adverb to tell how the phrase is used.

1. Jacy went to the library. _____
2. She needed a book about gardening. _____
3. The shelves in the library contained many books. _____
4. She asked the librarian with blue shoes. _____
5. The librarian in the green dress was very helpful. _____
6. She taught Jacy about the library catalog. _____
7. The library catalog has a computer entry for every book. _____
8. The entries are organized in three groups. _____
9. Some gardening books were in the health section. _____
10. Jacy's trip to the library was a great success. _____
11. She took several books with her. _____
12. Jacy read them at home. _____
13. The window seat in the living room was her favorite spot. _____
14. Jacy looked out the window. _____
15. Her own garden by the backyard fence was dead. _____
16. The vegetables from last year's garden had been delicious. _____
17. She would plant more vegetables near the house. _____
18. Then she would have many vegetables in the summer. _____

Name _____ Date _____

Conjunctions

- A **conjunction** is a word used to join words or groups of words.
  EXAMPLES:
  Shawn **and** Harris worked late.
  We worked **until** he arrived.
- These are some commonly used conjunctions:

although	because	however	or	that	until	whether
and	but	if	since	though	when	while
as	for	nor	than	unless	whereas	yet

- Some conjunctions are used in pairs. These include either . . . or, neither . . . nor, and not only . . . but also.

 Underline each conjunction in the sentences below.

1. We waited until the mechanic replaced the part.
2. Plums and peaches are my favorite fruits.
3. The wind blew, and the rain fell.
4. Please call Allen or Grant for me.
5. A conjunction may connect words or groups of words.
6. Cotton and wheat are grown on nearby farms.
7. Neither Anna nor Bonnie is my cousin.
8. Their home is not large, but it is comfortable.
9. Ron and Roy arrived on time.
10. Do not move the vase, for you may drop it.

 Complete each sentence with a conjunction.

11. I cannot leave _____ the babysitter arrives.

12. We must hurry, _____ we'll be late for work.

13. Battles were fought on the sea, on the land, _____ in the air.

14. Chet _____ Raul went to the movie, _____ Lester did not.

15. Please wait _____ Eliza gets ready.

16. Juan _____ I will carry that box upstairs.

17. Pete _____ Dan are twins.

18. We will stay home _____ you cannot go.

19. This nation exports cotton _____ wheat.

20. _____ the children _____ the parents liked the violent movie.

Name _____ Date _____

Interjections

- An **interjection** is a word or group of words that expresses emotion.
  EXAMPLE: **Hurrah!** Our team has won the game.
- If the interjection is used to express sudden or strong feeling, it is followed by an exclamation mark.
  EXAMPLE: **Wow!** You've really done it this time.
- If the interjection is used to express mild emotion, it is followed by a comma.
  EXAMPLE: **Oh,** I see what you mean.
- These are some commonly used interjections:

ah	good grief	oh	ugh
aha	great	oops	well
alas	hurrah	sh	whew

 Write sentences with the following interjections.

1. Ah _____
2. Wow _____
3. Oh _____
4. Ugh _____
5. Ouch _____
6. Oops _____
7. Hurrah _____
8. Oh, no _____
9. Hey _____
10. Sh _____
11. Help _____
12. Well _____
13. Whew _____
14. Oh, my _____
15. Hush _____
16. Hooray _____
17. Aha _____
18. Ha _____

Unit 3: Grammar and Usage

Name _____ Date _____

Unit 3 Test

Darken the circle by the kind of noun that is underlined in each sentence.

1. Our <u>vacation</u> was wonderful. Ⓐ common Ⓑ proper Ⓒ possessive
2. The judge told <u>Mr. Clark</u> he was free to go. Ⓐ common Ⓑ proper Ⓒ possessive
3. My <u>brother's</u> ranch is in Wyoming. Ⓐ common Ⓑ proper Ⓒ possessive

Darken the circle by the correct form of the noun.

4. singular Ⓐ men Ⓑ man Ⓒ men's
5. possessive Ⓐ brush Ⓑ brush's Ⓒ brushes
6. plural Ⓐ horse Ⓑ horses Ⓒ horse's

Darken the circle by each sentence with an appositive.

7. Ⓐ Grandma, please bake my favorite dessert.
   Ⓑ He told Eric, his brother, to be careful.
   Ⓒ Did you borrow my hat, Sharon?
   Ⓓ Hoover Dam took years to build.

8. Ⓐ Don't tell my secret, please.
   Ⓑ Finally, she remembered his name.
   Ⓒ No amount of time will ease the pain.
   Ⓓ The nurse, a young man, saved her life.

Darken the circle by the correct verb(s) to complete each sentence.

9. I _____ waiting here for an hour. Ⓐ been Ⓑ had Ⓒ have been
10. Did Kurt tell you that these _____ his photographs? Ⓐ was Ⓑ is Ⓒ are
11. He _____ work at the library this year. Ⓐ don't Ⓑ doesn't Ⓒ doing
12. _____ I have your new phone number? Ⓐ May Ⓑ Does Ⓒ Can
13. Can you _____ me how to play the guitar? Ⓐ learn Ⓑ learned Ⓒ teach
14. Will Joanna have time to _____ down before lunch? Ⓐ lie Ⓑ set Ⓒ lay
15. She _____ speak if there is time. Ⓐ may Ⓑ was Ⓒ is
16. Please _____ the book on the table. Ⓐ lie Ⓑ set Ⓒ sit
17. He said he _____ want any meat. Ⓐ don't Ⓑ doesn't Ⓒ do
18. It takes time to _____ something new. Ⓐ learn Ⓑ teach Ⓒ taught
19. _____ Lindsey going to pick up her package? Ⓐ Are Ⓑ Were Ⓒ Is
20. I am going to _____ down now. Ⓐ lie Ⓑ lay Ⓒ lying
21. She wants to _____ how to ski. Ⓐ teach Ⓑ learned Ⓒ learn
22. Jason _____ need anything from the store. Ⓐ do Ⓑ doesn't Ⓒ don't

Name _____ Date _____

Unit 3 Test, p. 2

Darken the circle by the correct past tense verb to complete each sentence.

23. Several of us ____ in a play. Ⓐ had sang   Ⓑ sung   Ⓒ have sung
24. I ____ my favorite vase yesterday. Ⓐ broke   Ⓑ had broke   Ⓒ broken
25. We ____ to the park for lunch. Ⓐ gone   Ⓑ went   Ⓒ have went
26. The bottle of soda ____. Ⓐ freezed   Ⓑ frozed   Ⓒ froze
27. She ____ out her old clothes. Ⓐ throw   Ⓑ thrown   Ⓒ threw
28. Who ____ this story? Ⓐ wrote   Ⓑ write   Ⓒ written
29. Tiffany ____ her a present. Ⓐ gived   Ⓑ gave   Ⓒ given

Darken the circle by the correct adjective or adverb to complete each sentence.

30. This is the ____ ice cream I've ever had. Ⓐ smoother   Ⓑ smoothest   Ⓒ most smooth
31. A squirrel can run ____ than a dog. Ⓐ quickest   Ⓑ quickly   Ⓒ more quickly

Darken the circle by the correct pronoun to complete each sentence.

32. Have you ever met ____ parents? Ⓐ hers   Ⓑ their   Ⓒ them
33. ____ was waiting for me when I got home. Ⓐ They   Ⓑ Both   Ⓒ No one
34. ____ and Laurel are going to the concert tonight. Ⓐ He   Ⓑ Him   Ⓒ Her
35. Please tell ____ to meet us at six o'clock. Ⓐ them   Ⓑ their   Ⓒ they
36. Chuck gave the prettiest flower to ____. Ⓐ she   Ⓑ hers   Ⓒ her
37. It was ____ who cooked the turkey. Ⓐ her   Ⓑ I   Ⓒ us
38. Leena chose ____ as her partner? Ⓐ whom   Ⓑ she   Ⓒ who

Darken the circle by the correct word to go with the article.

39. a   Ⓐ house   Ⓑ onion   Ⓒ umbrella
40. an   Ⓐ tomato   Ⓑ boat   Ⓒ icicle

Darken the circle by the way the prepositional phrase is used in the sentence.

41. I learned about outdoor safety <u>at a seminar</u>. Ⓐ as an adjective   Ⓑ as an adverb   Ⓒ not a prepositional phrase
42. We all liked our instructor <u>from England</u>. Ⓐ as an adjective   Ⓑ as an adverb   Ⓒ not a prepositional phrase
43. She was <u>very knowledgeable</u> about safety. Ⓐ as an adjective   Ⓑ as an adverb   Ⓒ not a prepositional phrase

Name _____ Date _____

Using Capital Letters

> • Capitalize the first word of a sentence.
>   EXAMPLE: **L**et's take a walk to the park.
> • Capitalize the first word of a quotation.
>   EXAMPLE: Joseph said, "**I**t's time for lunch."

 Circle each letter that should be capitalized. Write the capital letter above it.

1. haven't you made an appointment to meet them?
2. the teenagers will go to the game together.
3. danielle asked, "how did she like the book?"
4. the family moved to another state last year.
5. "bring your scripts to the practice," said the director.
6. who wrote this article for the newspaper?
7. the woman said, "my party is in one week."
8. "have some more carrot sticks," said the host.

> • Capitalize the first word of every line of poetry.
>   EXAMPLE: **T**he strong winds whipped
>   **T**he sails of the ship
> • Capitalize the first, last, and all important words in the titles of books, poems, songs, and stories.
>   EXAMPLES: *Gone with the Wind*   "America the Beautiful"

 Circle each letter that should be capitalized. Write the capital letter above it.

9. i eat my peas with honey;

   i've done it all my life.

   it makes the peas taste funny,

   but it keeps them on the knife!

10. it's midnight, and the setting sun

    is slowly rising in the west;

    the rapid rivers slowly run,

    the frog is on his downy nest.

11. Who wrote the poem "the children's hour"?
12. My favorite novel is *a wrinkle in time*.
13. The high school band played "stand by me."
14. During the summer, Kim read *adam of the road*.
15. Carla gave her poem the title "chasing the wind."

Name _____   Date _____

Using Capital Letters, p. 2

- Capitalize all proper nouns.
    EXAMPLES: Sarah, Dad, Arbor Street, England, Maine, Arctic Ocean, Ural Mountains, Columbus Day, February, Academy School, *Titanic*
- Capitalize all proper adjectives. A proper adjective is an adjective that is made from a proper noun.
    EXAMPLES: the Spanish language, American food, Chinese people

 Rewrite the following paragraph. Be sure to add capital letters where they are needed.

16. chris and her friends went to a festival in chicago, illinois. Some of them tasted greek pastry and canadian cheese soup. charley thought that the italian sausage and mexican tacos were delicious! laurel tried an unusual japanese salad. They all watched some irish folk dancers and listened to german music.

_____
_____
_____
_____
_____
_____
_____
_____
_____

 Circle each letter that should be capitalized. Write the capital letter above it.

17. Did anita and her family drive through arizona, new mexico, and colorado?

18. Isn't brazil larger in area than the united states?

19. Did mark twain live in the small town of hannibal, missouri?

20. Have you read the story of martin luther king?

21. I have been reading about the solomon islands.

22. The north sea is connected to the english channel by the strait of dover.

23. At thirteen, sam houston moved to tennessee from lexington, virginia.

24. Isn't st. augustine the oldest city in the united states?

25. Is nairobi the capital of kenya?

26. Our friend brought japanese money back from her trip.

Using Capital Letters, p. 3

> • Capitalize a person's title when it comes before a name.
>   EXAMPLES: Doctor Baker; Governor Alvarez; Senator Washington
> • Capitalize abbreviations of titles.
>   EXAMPLES: Dr. Garcia; Supt. Barbara Shurna; Mr. J. Howell, Sr.

 Circle each letter that should be capitalized. Write the capital letter above it.

27. Did captain cheng congratulate sergeant walters on his promotion?

28. The new health plan was developed by dr. ruth banks and mr. juan gomez.

29. After an introduction, pres. alice slater presented the next speaker, mr. gerald norman.

30. When did principal grissom invite mayor hadley to attend the graduation ceremony?

31. Officer halpern was the first to stand up when judge patterson entered the courtroom.

32. How long has mrs. frank been working for president howell?

33. Does prof. mary schneider teach this course, or does dr. david towne?

34. Prince andrew of england will tour the southern states in the fall.

35. Senator alan howell is the uncle of supt. joyce randall.

> • Capitalize abbreviations of days and months, parts of addresses, and titles of members of the armed forces. Also capitalize all letters in abbreviations for states.
>   EXAMPLES: Fri.; Jan.; 3720 E. Franklin Ave.; Gen. H. J. Farrimond; Los Angeles, CA; Dallas, TX

 Circle each letter that should be capitalized. Write the capital letter above it.

36. capt. margaret k. hansen
    2075 lakeview st.
    phoenix, az 85072

37. jackson school Track Meet
    at wilson stadium
    tues., sept. 26, 10:30
    649 n. clark blvd.

38. mr. jonathan bernt
    150 telson rd.
    markham, ontario L3R 1E5

39. lt. gary x. louis
    5931 congress rd.
    syracuse, ny 13217

40. thanksgiving Concert
    wed., nov. 23, 11:00
    Practice tues., nov. 22, 3:30
    See ms. evans for details.

41. gen. david grimes
    329 n. hayes st.
    louisville, ky 40227

Using End Punctuation

- Use a **period** at the end of a declarative sentence.
    EXAMPLE: Theresa's aunt lives in Florida.
- Use a **question mark** at the end of an interrogative sentence.
    EXAMPLE: Will you carry this package for me?

 Use a period or question mark to end each sentence below.

1. Ms. Clark has moved her law office____
2. Isn't this Lance's baseball glove____
3. Are you moving to Massachusetts next month____
4. It's too late to buy tickets for the game____
5. Our program will begin in five minutes____
6. Does your sister drive a truck____
7. Ms. Tobin's store was damaged by the flood____
8. Are you going to Reba's party____
9. Luci did not take the plane to St. Petersburg____
10. Do you have a stamp for this envelope____
11. Have you ever seen Clara laugh so hard____
12. President Sophia Harris called the meeting to order____
13. Will Gilmore Plumbing be open on Labor Day____
14. School ends the second week in June____
15. We are going camping in Canada this summer____

 Add the correct end punctuation where needed in the paragraph below.

Have you ever been to the Olympic Games____ If not, have you ever seen them on television____ I hope to see them in person someday____ The Olympic Games are held every four years in a different country____ The games started in ancient Greece, but the games as we now know them date back to 1896____ Some of the finest athletes in the world compete for bronze, silver, and gold medals____ Can you think of a famous Olympic athlete____ What is your favorite Olympic sport____ It could be a winter or summer sport because the games are held for each season____ One U.S. athlete won seven gold medals in swimming at one Olympics____ Can you imagine how excited that athlete must have felt, knowing that he had represented the United States so well____ That is the U.S. record to date____ However, there will be plenty more chances for that record to be broken____

Name _____ Date _____

Using End Punctuation, p. 2

- Use a period at the end of an imperative sentence.
    EXAMPLE: Close the door to the attic.
- Use an **exclamation point** at the end of an exclamatory sentence and after an interjection that shows strong feelings.
    EXAMPLES: What a great shot! I'd love to go with you! Wow!

 Add periods and exclamation points where needed in the sentences below.

16. Address the envelope to Dr. George K. Zimmerman___
17. How nicely dressed you are___
18. Hurry___ The bus is ready to leave___
19. Get some paints for your next art lesson___
20. Shake hands with Mr. D. B. Norton___
21. Oops___ I spilled the glass of orange juice___
22. Carry this bag to the car in the parking lot___
23. What a great view you have from your apartment window___
24. Wipe the counter when you're through eating___
25. Oh, what a beautiful painting___
26. I can't wait until summer vacation___
27. Please take this to the post office for me___
28. Just look at the size of the fish he caught___
29. I've never seen a larger one___
30. Get the net from under the life preserver___
31. I hope the pictures come out well___

 Add the correct end punctuation where needed in the paragraph below.

The state of Maine in New England is a wonderful place to visit in the summer or winter___ Have you ever been there___ It is best known for its rocky coastline on the Atlantic Ocean___ Visitors often drive along the rugged coast___ There are numerous quaint sea towns along the coast that date back to the 1600s___ What a long time ago that was___ Mount Katahdin and the northern part of the Appalachian Mountains are ideal places for winter sports, such as downhill and cross-country skiing___ If you've never seen a deer or moose, you'd probably see plenty of them while hiking in Acadia National Park___ It has over 30,000 acres___ Do you know anything about Maine's local fish___ Well, there are many kinds that are native to its rivers and lakes___ But Maine is famous for its Atlantic lobsters___ Rockport and Rockland are two of the largest cities for lobster fishing___ Lobsters from northern Maine are flown all over the world___ Blueberries are another big product of Maine___ Have you ever had wild blueberries___ Some people consider them to be the best___

Name _____   Date _____

Using Commas

> - Use a **comma** between words or groups of words in a series.
>   EXAMPLE: Be sure your business letter is brief, courteous, and correct.
> - Use a comma before a conjunction in a compound sentence.
>   EXAMPLE: Neal sketched the cartoon, and Claire wrote the caption.

 Add commas where needed in the sentences below.

1. The United States exports cotton corn and wheat to many countries.
2. The children played softball ran races and pitched horseshoes.
3. Lauren held the nail and Tasha hit it with a hammer.
4. Alex Henry Carmen and Jamie go to the library often.
5. The pitcher threw a fastball and the batter struck out.
6. Sara peeled the peaches and Reggie sliced them.
7. The mountains were covered with forests of pine cedar and oak.
8. Craig should stop running or he will be out of breath.
9. Baseball is Lee's favorite sport but Vince's favorite is football.
10. Limestone marble granite and slate are found in Vermont New Hampshire and Maine.
11. The rain fell steadily and the lightning flashed.
12. Mindy enjoyed the corn but Frank preferred the string beans.

> - Use a comma to set off a quotation from the rest of a sentence.
>   EXAMPLES: "We must get up early," said Mom.
>   Mom said, "We must get up early."

 Add commas before or after the quotations below.

13. "Please show me how this machine works" said Karla.
14. "Be sure you keep your eyes on the road" said the driving instructor.
15. Rick replied "I can't believe my ears."
16. Gail said "Travel is dangerous on the icy roads."
17. "Paul studied piano for two years" said Ms. Walters.
18. Alex said "That goat eats everything in sight."
19. "Let's go to the park for a picnic" said Rosa.
20. "Wait for me here" said Randy.
21. Luke said "Sandy, thank you for the present."
22. "I'm going to the game with Alberto" remarked Frank.
23. Alberto asked "What time should we leave?"
24. Chris remembered "I was only five when we moved to New York."

Unit 4: Capitalization and Punctuation

Name _____ Date _____

Using Commas, p. 2

> - Use a comma to set off the name of a person who is being addressed.
>   EXAMPLE: Angela, did you find the answer to your question?
> - Use a comma to set off words like <u>yes</u>, <u>no</u>, <u>well</u>, and <u>oh</u> at the beginning of a sentence.
>   EXAMPLE: No, I haven't seen Jackson today.
> - Use a comma to set off an appositive.
>   EXAMPLE: Marshall, Mary's brother, is going to college next fall.

 Add commas where needed in the sentences below.

25. Miss Hunt do you know the answer to that question?
26. Can't you find the book I brought you last week Roger?
27. Dr. Levin the Smiths' dentist sees patients on weekends.
28. Oh I guess it takes about an hour to get to Denver.
29. Dad may Sam and I go to the ball game?
30. Our neighbor Will Johnson is a carpenter.
31. What is the population of your city Leann?
32. Well I'm not sure of the exact number.
33. Britney are you going skiing this weekend?
34. What time are you going to the concert Greg?
35. Otto our friend coaches the softball team.
36. Susan have you seen a small black cat around your neighborhood?
37. Jeff do you know Mr. D. B. Norton?
38. No I don't think we've ever met.
39. Janna and John would you like to go shopping on Saturday?
40. Mrs. Porter the principal is retiring this year.
41. Yes the teachers are planning a retirement dinner for her.
42. Mrs. Porter and her husband Hal plan to move to Oregon.

 Add commas where needed in the paragraph below.

I have two friends who are always there for me and I tell them everything. So it was a surprise to me when Kathy my oldest friend said "Well when are you moving?" I said "What do you mean?" She said "I don't believe you our dearest friend wouldn't tell us first what was going on in your life." Marcy my other friend said "I feel the same way. Anna why on Earth did we have to hear about this from Leroy?" "Marcy and Kathy I don't know what you're talking about" I said. "Oh don't be ashamed" said Marcy. "We know you must have some good reason and we're waiting to hear it." "No I don't have any reason because I'm not moving" I said. "Leroy that prankster must have been trying to play a joke on us" said Kathy.

Using Quotation Marks and Apostrophes

- Use **quotation marks** to show the exact words of a speaker.
- Use a comma or another punctuation mark to separate the quotation from the rest of the sentence.
    EXAMPLES: "Do you have a book on helicopters?" asked Thomas.
             Jeremy said, "It's right here."
- A quotation may be placed at the beginning or at the end of a sentence. It may also be divided within the sentence.
    EXAMPLES: Deborah said, "There are sixty active members."
             "Morton," asked Juanita, "have you read this magazine article?"

 Add quotation marks and other punctuation where needed in the sentences below.

1. Dan, did you ever play football asked Tom.
2. Morris asked Why didn't you come in for an interview?
3. I have never heard a story said Laurie about a ghost.
4. Selina said Yuri thank you for the present.
5. When do we start on our trip to the mountains asked Stan.
6. Our guest said You don't know how happy I am to be in your house.
7. My sister said Kelly bought those beautiful baskets in Mexico.
8. I'm going to plant the spinach said Doris as soon as I get home.

- Use an **apostrophe** in a contraction to show where a letter or letters have been taken out.
    EXAMPLES: Amelia **didn't** answer the phone.
             I've found my wallet.
- Use an apostrophe to form a possessive noun. Add 's to most singular nouns. Add ' to most plural nouns. Add 's to a few nouns that have irregular plurals.
    EXAMPLES: A **child's** toy was in our yard.
             The **girls'** toys were in our yard.
             The **children's** toys were in our yard.

 After each sentence below, write the word in which an apostrophe has been left out. Add the apostrophe where needed.

9. Many players uniforms are red. _____

10. That dog played with the babys shoe. _____

11. Julio isnt coming with us to the library. _____

12. Its very warm for a fall day. _____

13. The captains ship was one of the newest. _____

14. Marcia doesnt sing as well as my sister does. _____

15. Mens coats are sold in the new store. _____

Name _____ Date _____

Using Colons and Hyphens

- Use a **colon** after the greeting in a business letter.
    EXAMPLES: Dear Sir: Dear Ms. Franklin:
- Use a colon between the hour and the minute when writing time.
    EXAMPLES: 2:00   7:45   9:37
- Use a colon to introduce a list.
    EXAMPLE: The suitcase contained these items: a toothbrush, a brush, a comb, and some clothing.

 Add colons where needed in the sentences or phrases below.

1. The program begins at 8 3 0.
2. Dear Mrs. Sanchez
3. These are the students who must return library books Julia Turner, Carl Porter, Crystal Fletcher, and Asako Satoshi.
4. Beverly wakes up every morning at 6 1 5.
5. Dear Mr. Graham

- Use a **hyphen** between the parts of some compound words.
    EXAMPLES: father-in-law   blue-black   well-known   thirty-six
- Use a hyphen to separate the syllables of a word that is carried over from one line to the next.
    EXAMPLE: After eating dinner, we watched a television show about tornadoes in the Midwest.

 Add hyphens where needed in the sentences below.

6. A driving safety expert will visit the school to give a presen tation on seat belts.
7. There should be forty two people at the lecture.
8. I searched high and low, but I couldn't seem to find that new, yellow zip per I bought today.
9. My mother in law is coming from Florida.
10. In fifty eight years of driving, he has a nearly perfect record.
11. Ralph and Victor came late to the meeting, but Lora and Angela arrived ear ly and stayed late.
12. George could lift weights with ease, and Alberto was able to swim twenty one laps without stopping.
13. Our air conditioning unit broke on the hottest day of this summer.
14. Donna had to go inside to change her clothes because Scoot, her frisky pup py, got his muddy paws on her.

Name _____   Date _____

Unit 4 Test

Darken the circle by the word in each sentence that should be capitalized.

1. I had sweet and sour chicken at a chinese restaurant.
   - Ⓐ sweet
   - Ⓑ chicken
   - Ⓒ chinese
   - Ⓓ restaurant

2. My parents celebrated their wedding anniversary in may.
   - Ⓐ parents
   - Ⓑ wedding
   - Ⓒ anniversary
   - Ⓓ may

3. Who wrote the adventure story *The Call of the wild*?
   - Ⓐ wrote
   - Ⓑ adventure
   - Ⓒ story
   - Ⓓ wild

4. I met mayor Bradley at the celebration yesterday.
   - Ⓐ met
   - Ⓑ mayor
   - Ⓒ celebration
   - Ⓓ yesterday

5. She lives at 503 north Bryer Street, on the corner near the store.
   - Ⓐ corner
   - Ⓑ store
   - Ⓒ north
   - Ⓓ near

6. The earthquake shook the ground in Los Angeles, california.
   - Ⓐ california
   - Ⓑ earthquake
   - Ⓒ ground
   - Ⓓ shook

Darken the circle by the correct answer to the question.

In which sentences are commas used correctly?

7.
   - Ⓐ I called, but Amy wasn't home.
   - Ⓑ We ate cheese, apples and bread.
   - Ⓒ "No" she said "I, can't go."
   - Ⓓ The answer is, that we just don't know.

8.
   - Ⓐ Stop look, and listen Bob.
   - Ⓑ "We would like to go," said Hans.
   - Ⓒ Enrique, my friend lives, in Houston.
   - Ⓓ My arm hurts but, it's okay.

9.
   - Ⓐ My best friend, Pat and I can come.
   - Ⓑ Tell me now, what you want.
   - Ⓒ Well, yes, I do like spinach.
   - Ⓓ I left and then, Karen went home.

10.
    - Ⓐ Tanya, did you see the show?
    - Ⓑ Becka asked "How are you, Eric?"
    - Ⓒ Well, how will you get there Jay?
    - Ⓓ She told the truth, and was not believed.

Darken the circle by the correct answer to the question.

In which sentences is end punctuation used correctly?

11.
    - Ⓐ How wonderful our trip was?
    - Ⓑ I can't remember.
    - Ⓒ Are you going to the fair!
    - Ⓓ I just love this book so much.

12.
    - Ⓐ Wow. That's a great album.
    - Ⓑ Can you go with us!
    - Ⓒ Have you seen a shooting star?
    - Ⓓ What a great ceremony?

13.
    - Ⓐ Take control of the car.
    - Ⓑ Please, will you come!
    - Ⓒ Don't I know you.
    - Ⓓ Let me read that first?

14.
    - Ⓐ That program was awful?
    - Ⓑ Could you hear her sing!
    - Ⓒ Let me watch for them.
    - Ⓓ Ouch. That hurt.

Name _____ Date _____

Unit 4 Test, p. 2

Darken the circle by the correct answers to the questions.

In which sentences are quotation marks used correctly?

15. Ⓐ "No," said Ted, "I can't go.
    Ⓑ "Are you leaving?" asked Leon.
    Ⓒ "Yes, said Jacob, I am."
    Ⓓ Shawna said, Be sure to write!"

16. Ⓐ "How are you"? asked Dan.
    Ⓑ "How, asked Sue, do you do it?"
    Ⓒ "When can you come?" I asked.
    Ⓓ "Yes! said Marie, "I can."

17. Ⓐ For now, I'll just wait," said Todd.
    Ⓑ "Why don't you ask? said Luis.
    Ⓒ "Please let me in!" said Carmen.
    Ⓓ "No, said Jeff, "I'm not ready yet."

18. Ⓐ Brent said, "Throw that away."
    Ⓑ "It's still good, said Rebecca."
    Ⓒ "Now," said Lily, just watch me!"
    Ⓓ "Don't forget to jump, said Ruth.

In which sentences are apostrophes used correctly?

19. Ⓐ I ca'nt meet you until 6:30.
    Ⓑ Il'l walk the dog.
    Ⓒ It's 12:00, and I am late!
    Ⓓ The dog shook it's head.

20. Ⓐ I'm sorry I can't be there.
    Ⓑ Lets' go together.
    Ⓒ I need two day's notice.
    Ⓓ W'ere all staying home.

21. Ⓐ Tell them the'yre almost here.
    Ⓑ Our neighbor's party was loud.
    Ⓒ Two trees' caught on fire.
    Ⓓ Listen to the'ir reasons.

22. Ⓐ The picture tell's the story.
    Ⓑ I love Charlotte's home.
    Ⓒ His cats' were both black.
    Ⓓ The papers have'nt been delivered.

Darken the circle by the correct answers to the questions.

In which sentences or phrases are colons used correctly?

23. Ⓐ Dear Mom:
    Ⓑ Sincerely yours:
    Ⓒ 10:30 P.M.
    Ⓓ 615 A.M.

24. Ⓐ Take these things: a book, a pen, and some paper.
    Ⓑ Leave the house by 1130, or you'll be late.
    Ⓒ Don't worry: I'm fine.
    Ⓓ She called the following: names.

25. Ⓐ Dear Sir:
    Ⓑ The play begins at 83:0.
    Ⓒ Please: use this door.
    Ⓓ Thank you: for all your help.

In which sentences are hyphens used correctly?

26. Ⓐ My father-in-law came to visit.
    Ⓑ My part time-job is fun.
    Ⓒ There were more than thirty two-people.
    Ⓓ One half-of the cake was eaten.

27. Ⓐ Dorothy was fif-teen minutes late.
    Ⓑ A firefighter gave a presenta-tion on fire safety.
    Ⓒ Twenty six-pizzas were delivered to the party.
    Ⓓ That monument is over one-hundred years old.

28. Ⓐ The air conditioner was-broken.
    Ⓑ She is twenty-one years old.
    Ⓒ The sun-set was orange red.
    Ⓓ He likes his sister in-law.

Name _____ Date _____

Writing Sentences

- Every sentence has a base consisting of a simple subject and a simple predicate.
    EXAMPLE: Dolphins leap.
- Expand the meaning of a sentence by adding adjectives, adverbs, and prepositional phrases to the sentence base.
    EXAMPLE: **The sleek** dolphins **suddenly** leap **high into the air**.

 Expand the meaning of each sentence base by adding adjectives, adverbs, and/or prepositional phrases. Write each expanded sentence.

1. (Sister cooks.) _____
2. (Clown chuckled.) _____
3. (Car raced.) _____
4. (Dancer spun.) _____
5. (Panthers growled.) _____
6. (Leaves fall.) _____
7. (Bread tasted.) _____
8. (Lake glistened.) _____
9. (Ship glides.) _____

Write five sentence bases. Then write an expanded sentence containing each sentence base.

10. _____
    _____

11. _____
    _____

12. _____
    _____

13. _____
    _____

14. _____
    _____

Name _____ Date _____

Writing Topic Sentences

> - A **topic sentence** is the sentence within a paragraph that states the main idea.
> - It is often placed at the beginning of a paragraph.
>   EXAMPLE:
>   **The trip to the national park was a great success.** First, the visitors learned a lot from their guide about the park. They learned that the forest was created by people, not by nature. To their surprise, they found out that the park had more than five hundred species of plants. Then they went on a hike and even spotted a falcon flying overhead. Finally, the visitors had a wonderful picnic lunch and headed back home.

 Write a topic sentence for each paragraph below.

1. Some jewelry is made out of feathers, leather, shells, or wood. Other jewelry is crafted from gold, silver, brass, copper, or other metals. Gems and unusual stones are added for their beauty and value.

   Topic Sentence: _____

2. A pet goldfish needs clean water. A pump should be placed in the water to supply fresh air. The water temperature must be constant, and it must not go below 27°C (80°F). The goldfish should be fed flaked fish food or small insects.

   Topic Sentence: _____

3. When Jana crawls over to a kitchen cabinet, she whips the door open to see what's behind it. With a little help from Jana, the pots and pans are on the floor in no time. If she sees a bag of groceries, Jana has to investigate the contents. After she is tucked in bed for the night, this toddler loves to climb out of her crib and explore.

   Topic Sentence: _____

 Write a topic sentence for each of the paragraph ideas below.

4. birthday parties _____

5. a great adventure _____

6. a great president _____

7. a favorite holiday _____

8. homework _____

9. video games _____

10. vacations _____

11. the Olympics _____

Name _____ Date _____

Writing Supporting Details

- The idea expressed in a topic sentence can be developed with sentences containing **supporting details**.
- Details can include facts, examples, and reasons.

 Read the topic sentence below. Then read the sentences that follow. Circle the seven sentences that contain details that support the topic sentence.

Topic Sentence: The Big Dipper Theme Park is a wonderful place to go for a fun-filled day.

1. The roller coaster is the most popular ride in the park.
2. The park was built in 1959.
3. You can test your pitching skills at the game booths.
4. You can win a stuffed animal at one of the pitching games.
5. Young children can enjoy a part of the park made especially for them.
6. We had sandwiches and potato salad for lunch.
7. The train ride is a pleasant way to relax and see the park.
8. However, the water rides are a great way to beat the heat.
9. What do you like to do during summer vacation?
10. The sky ride provides a grand tour of the park from high in the air.

 Choose one of the topic sentences below. Write it on the first line. Then write five sentences that contain supporting details. The details can be facts, examples, or reasons.

a. Exercise is important for maintaining good health.
b. Being the oldest child in a family has its advantages.
c. The teenage years are a time of change.
d. True friendship makes life more interesting and fun.

_____
_____
_____
_____
_____
_____
_____
_____

Name _____ Date _____

Topic and Audience

- The **topic** of a paragraph is the subject of the paragraph.
- The **title** of a paragraph should be based on the topic.
- The **audience** is the person or persons who will read the paragraph.
    EXAMPLES: teachers, classmates, readers of the school newspaper, friends, family members

 Suppose that you chose the topic watching TV. Underline the sentence that you would choose for the topic sentence.

   a. Watching TV is one of the best ways to learn about things.

   b. Watching TV is a waste of time.

   c. The time children spend watching TV should be limited.

 Think about the topic sentence you chose above. Then underline the audience for whom you would like to write.

   1. your friends

   2. your family members

   3. readers of a newspaper

Write a paragraph beginning with the topic sentence you chose above. Keep your chosen audience in mind as you write. Be sure to write a title.

Name _____ Date _____

Taking Notes

- **Note taking** is an important step when writing a report.
- You can find information for reports in encyclopedias, books, and magazines.
- Before you begin, organize your research questions.
- Write information accurately and in your own words.
- Take more notes than you expect to need, so you won't have to go back to your sources a second time.

 Underline a topic below that interests you.

1. a favorite hobby
2. the stars or planets
3. a historical figure
4. a species of animal
5. movies

6. a favorite sport
7. a favorite food
8. fashion or costumes
9. gardening
10. airplanes

 Gather some sources of information about your topic. Write the name of your topic on the first line below. For example, if you have chosen "a favorite food," you might write the name of that particular food. Then write notes about the topic on the remaining lines.

_____

_____
_____
_____
_____
_____
_____
_____
_____
_____
_____
_____
_____
_____

Name _____ Date _____

Outlining

- Organize your thoughts before writing by making an **outline**.
- An outline consists of the **title** of the topic, **main headings** for the main ideas, and **subheadings** for the supporting ideas.
- Main headings are listed after Roman numerals. Subheadings are listed after capital letters.

Topic: First aid for burns

Main heading   I. Keeping the wound clean
Subheadings {   A. Applying thick, clean dressing
               B. Avoiding sprays or oils
         II. Easing pain
            A. Applying ice packs
            B. Putting injured area in ice water

 Write an outline for the topic you chose on page 101. Use the sample outline above as a guide.

Topic: _____

I. _____
     A. _____
     B. _____

II. _____
     A. _____
     B. _____

III. _____
     A. _____
     B. _____

IV. _____
     A. _____
     B. _____

V. _____
     A. _____
     B. _____

Name _____ Date _____

Writing a Report

- A **report** is a series of informative paragraphs covering a main topic.
- Each paragraph has a topic sentence and other sentences that contain supporting details.
- Begin with a paragraph that introduces the report, and end with a paragraph that concludes the report.

 Read the paragraphs below.

Exploring the Mystery Planets: Uranus, Neptune, and Pluto

The planets Uranus, Neptune, and Pluto are difficult to study because of their distance from Earth. However, scientists are not completely without information about these planets. They know, for example, that Uranus is more than twice as far from Earth as Saturn is. They also know that Neptune is half again as far from Earth as Uranus. Both Saturn and Uranus are four times the size of Earth.

Scientists have explored the mysteries of Uranus. As Uranus orbits the sun every 84 years, it rolls around on its side. Although it is larger than Earth and orbits the sun more slowly, Uranus spins on its axis very rapidly. It completes a full rotation in 15 hours, 30 minutes. Five known satellites accompany Uranus, along with a system of nine dark rings that were discovered in 1977. The diameter of Uranus is 32,500 miles (52,200 kilometers), and the planet lies 1.78 billion miles (2.87 billion kilometers) from the sun. Because of this great distance, the temperature of Uranus is –360°F (– 220°C), far too cold for any Earth creature to survive.

Scientists have also explored the mysteries of Neptune. At a distance of 2.8 billion miles (4.5 billion kilometers) from the sun, Neptune appears through a telescope as a greenish-blue disc. Neptune is somewhat smaller than Uranus, having a diameter of about 30,000 miles (48,600 kilometers). It is also very cold (– 328°F, or – 200°C). Two of Neptune's satellites have been named Nereid and Triton. In the summer of 1989, *Voyager 2* finally passed Neptune and, among other things, revealed that there are up to five rings around the planet.

It was 1930 before Pluto, the last planet in our solar system, was discovered. The "new" planet is 3.67 billion miles (6 billion kilometers) from the sun and takes 248 years to complete its orbit. In comparison, Earth takes only 365 days to complete a single orbit. While Pluto has not been measured exactly, scientists believe that it has a diameter of 1,600 miles (2,670 kilometers).

There are more interesting facts about Pluto. It also has a satellite, called Charon, which is five times closer to Pluto than our moon is to Earth. The yellowish color of Pluto indicates that it has very little atmosphere. Pluto's distance from the sun indicates that its climate is the coldest of the nine planets in our solar system.

Many mysteries remain concerning Uranus, Neptune, and Pluto, despite the fact that so much has been discovered. The questioning minds of the twenty-first century will continue our search for the secrets of space.

 Circle the word or phrase that best completes each statement about this report.

1. Most of the report's supporting details are (facts, examples, reasons).

2. The writer of this report has included the (color, discoverer, diameter) of each of the three planets.

3. The writer does not discuss the relationship of the mystery planets to (Earth, Mars, the sun).

 Underline the topic sentence in each paragraph.

Name _____ Date _____

Revising and Proofreading

- **Revising** gives you a chance to rethink and review what you have written and to improve your writing.
- Revise by adding or removing words and moving words, sentences, and paragraphs around.
- **Proofreading** has to do with checking spelling, punctuation, grammar, and capitalization.
- Use proofreader's marks to show changes needed in your writing.

Proofreader's Marks

Capitalize.	Add a period.	Correct spelling.
Make a small letter.	Add something.	Indent for new paragraph.
Add a comma.	Take something out.	Move something.

 Rewrite the paragraph below. Correct the errors by following the proofreader's marks.

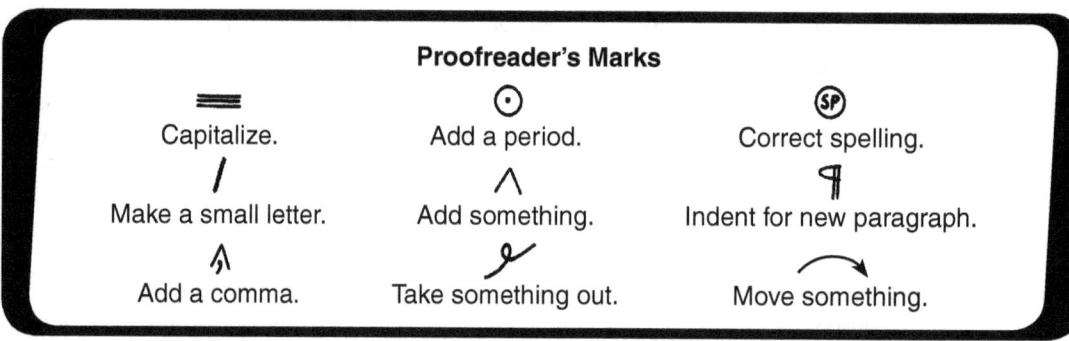

_____
_____
_____
_____
_____
_____
_____

Name _____ Date _____

Revising and Proofreading, p. 2

 Read the paragraphs below. Use proofreader's marks to revise and proofread the paragraphs. Then write your revised paragraphs below.

although yellowstons national park is the largest national national park in the United states, other national parks are also well-known yosemite national park in california has acres of Mountain Scenery and miles of hiking trails. Won of the world's largest biggest waterfalls can also be found in yosemite.

mammoth cave national park in kentucky features a huge underground cave the cave over has 212 miles of corridors it also have underground lakes rivers and waterfalls this cave system is estimated to be millions of years old

many pepul are surprized to learn that their are national parks in alaska and hawaii. mount McKinley the highest mountain in north america is located in denali national park in alaska. you can travel to hawaii and visit hawaii volcanoes national park this Park Has too active volcanoes rare plants and animals.

_____
_____
_____
_____
_____
_____
_____
_____
_____
_____
_____
_____

Name _____ Date _____

Writing a Business Letter

A **business letter** has six parts.
- The **heading** contains the address of the person writing and the date.
- The **inside address** contains the name and address of the person to whom the letter is written.
- The **greeting** tells to whom the letter is written. Use "Dear Sir or Madam" if you are unsure who will read the letter. Use a colon after the greeting in a business letter.
- The **body** is the message of the letter. It should be brief, courteous, and to the point.
- The **closing** is the ending that follows the body.
- The **signature** is the name of the person who is writing the letter.

When writing a business letter, remember the following:
- Use business-size paper and envelopes.
- Center your letter on the page, leaving at least a one-inch margin on each side.
- Include specific information, such as quantities, sizes, numbers, brands, prices, manner of shipment, and amount of payment.
- When you have finished, reread your letter. Rewrite it if you are not satisfied with any part of it.

 Study this business letter. Then answer the questions below.

heading	572 Ironwood Avenue Orlando, FL 32887 April 4, 2007
inside address	Order Department Perfection Computer Company 9940 Main Street Brooklyn, NY 11227

greeting
body
	Dear Sir or Madam:
	   Please send me one copy of <u>Making Friends With Your Computer</u>. Enclosed is $16.95 to cover the cost of the book plus shipping and handling.
	   Thank you for your assistance.

closing signature	Sincerely yours, *Chris Morrow* Chris Morrow

1. Who wrote the letter? _____

2. What is the greeting? _____

3. Where is Perfection Computer Company located? _____

4. When was the letter written? _____

Name _____ Date _____

Writing a Business Letter, p. 2

- Use a business-size envelope to send a business letter.
- Be sure to include your return address.
- Check both addresses to be sure they are correct.

Chris Morrow
572 Ironwood Avenue
Orlando, FL 32887

                    Order Department
                    Perfection Computer Company
                    9940 Main Street
                    Brooklyn, NY 11227

Write a brief business letter asking for information about the Chicago Fire that you can use in a report. Write to the Chicago Historical Society at 1601 North Clark Street in Chicago, Illinois. The zip code is 60616. Then circle the parts of the letter that would appear on the envelope.

_____
_____
_____
_____
_____
_____
_____
_____
_____
_____
_____
_____
_____
_____
_____

Name _____ Date _____

Unit 5 Test

Read the paragraph. Then darken the circle by the correct answer to each question.

You probably know that many kinds of penguins live in very cold places. In fact, some types of penguins actually lay their eggs on ice. Fortunately, penguins have thick layers of fat that help keep them warm. Some male penguins have extra rolls of fat, which they use to keep the eggs and later the newly hatched baby penguins warm. Originally, penguins were capable of flying, but millions of years ago their wings became more like flippers. They use their small wings as paddles for swimming. One of the most interesting things about penguins is the way they waddle on their extremely short legs.

1. Which sentence can best be used as a topic sentence for the paragraph above?
   - Ⓐ Penguins like cold weather.
   - Ⓑ Male penguins care for their young.
   - Ⓒ The penguin is an unusual bird.
   - Ⓓ Penguins lay eggs.

2. Which sentence would be the best supporting detail for the paragraph above?
   - Ⓐ Penguins live in the southern half of the world.
   - Ⓑ Penguins are popular additions to most zoos.
   - Ⓒ All penguins are black and white.
   - Ⓓ The male penguin produces a milky substance in its throat, which it uses to feed its young.

3. Which audience would be the most interested in this paragraph?
   - Ⓐ grandparents
   - Ⓑ soccer coaches
   - Ⓒ animal lovers
   - Ⓓ nurses

Darken the circle by the sentence that does not contain details that support the topic sentence.

4. **Topic Sentence:** A chef's job is very demanding.
   - Ⓐ Great chefs can make very good money.
   - Ⓑ Chefs must cook many things at once.
   - Ⓒ They must make sure a party's meals are ready at the same time.
   - Ⓓ Chefs must cook food as quickly as possible.

5. **Topic Sentence:** Wild mustangs are increasing in number.
   - Ⓐ People with ranches are letting mustangs roam free.
   - Ⓑ Wild mustangs are smaller than other breeds.
   - Ⓒ Some people adopt wild mustangs and care for them.
   - Ⓓ More laws are in place to protect the mustangs.

Name _____   Date _____

Unit 5 Test, p. 2

Darken the circle by the correct answer to each question.

6. Which is not good advice for taking research notes?
   - Ⓐ Use reference materials for information.
   - Ⓑ Take notes and then organize research questions.
   - Ⓒ Always put information in your own words.
   - Ⓓ Take more notes than you expect to need.

7. Which is not part of an outline?
   - Ⓐ subheadings
   - Ⓑ title
   - Ⓒ main headings
   - Ⓓ introductory paragraph

8. Which is not part of a report?
   - Ⓐ title
   - Ⓑ main headings
   - Ⓒ topic sentences
   - Ⓓ informative paragraphs

9. Which is not part of a business letter?
   - Ⓐ body
   - Ⓑ heading
   - Ⓒ signature
   - Ⓓ title

10. Which is not part of writing a good business letter?
    - Ⓐ Reread and rewrite, if necessary.
    - Ⓑ Use the person's first name in the greeting.
    - Ⓒ Include specific information.
    - Ⓓ Use business-size paper and envelopes.

11. Which part of a business letter follows the body?
    - Ⓐ greeting
    - Ⓑ heading
    - Ⓒ inside address
    - Ⓓ closing

Darken the circle by the correct revision of each underlined sentence.

12. dr. Jones came, I and Paul visited with him
    - Ⓐ When Dr. Jones came Paul and I visited with him.
    - Ⓑ When Dr. Jones visited, I and Paul came with him.
    - Ⓒ Dr. Jones came, and Paul and I visited with him.
    - Ⓓ When Dr. Jones came, Paul and I visited with him.

13. tell Kay what that she herd was a the secret
    - Ⓐ Tell Kay, what she herd was the secret.
    - Ⓑ Tell Kay what she heard that was a secret.
    - Ⓒ Tell Kay that what she heard was a secret.
    - Ⓓ Tell Kay that what she heard.

14. the gold rush, people streamed form over all the country to Californa
    - Ⓐ All the people from the country streamed to California.
    - Ⓑ During the Gold Rush, people from all over streamed to California.
    - Ⓒ People streamed from all over the country to the Gold Rush.
    - Ⓓ During the Gold Rush, people from all over the country streamed to California.

Name _____ Date _____

Dictionary: Guide Words

- A **dictionary** is a reference book that contains definitions of words and other information about their history and use.
- **Entries** in a dictionary are listed in **alphabetical order**.
- **Guide words** appear at the top of each dictionary page. Guide words show the first and last entry on the page.
    EXAMPLE: The word dog would appear on a dictionary page with the guide words dodge / doll. The word dull would not.

✱ Put a check in front of each word that would be listed on the dictionary page with the given guide words.

1. frozen / gather
_____ fruit
_____ grain
_____ furnish
_____ gate
_____ gallon
_____ former
_____ forgive
_____ fuzz
_____ galaxy
_____ future

2. money / muscle
_____ muddy
_____ moss
_____ motorcycle
_____ mustard
_____ moisten
_____ moose
_____ museum
_____ morning
_____ mortal
_____ modest

3. perfect / pin
_____ perfume
_____ pit
_____ pick
_____ photo
_____ pest
_____ plastic
_____ pillow
_____ pile
_____ pipe
_____ pizza

✱ Number the words in each column in the order in which they would appear in a dictionary. Then write the words that could be the guide words for each column.

4. _____ / _____
_____ raccoon
_____ radar
_____ rabbit
_____ raisin
_____ react
_____ reflect
_____ rebel
_____ rainfall
_____ relay
_____ remind
_____ refuse
_____ ran

5. _____ / _____
_____ seize
_____ shellfish
_____ shrink
_____ signal
_____ silent
_____ scent
_____ shuffle
_____ shaft
_____ serpent
_____ seldom
_____ scope
_____ selfish

6. _____ / _____
_____ octopus
_____ olive
_____ of
_____ office
_____ old
_____ odor
_____ once
_____ oil
_____ odd
_____ onion
_____ occasion
_____ only

www.harcourtschoolsupply.com
© Harcourt Achieve Inc. All rights reserved.

Unit 6: Study Skills
Language: Usage and Practice 6, SV 1419027832

Name _____ Date _____

Dictionary: Syllables

- A **syllable** is a part of a word that is pronounced at one time.
- Dictionary entry words are divided into syllables to show how they can be divided at the end of a writing line.
- A **hyphen (-)** is placed between syllables to separate them.
  EXAMPLE: man-a-ger
- If a word has a beginning or ending syllable of only one letter, do not divide it at the end of a writing line so that one letter stands alone.
  EXAMPLES: a-lone   sand-y

✳ **Write each word as a whole word.**

1. ad-ver-tise _____
2. blun-der _____
3. par-a-dise _____
4. mis-chie-vous _____
5. con-crete _____
6. mi-cro-phone _____
7. in-ci-dent _____
8. val-ue _____

✳ **Find each word in a dictionary. Rewrite the word, placing a hyphen between each syllable.**

9. bicycle _____
10. solution _____
11. category _____
12. punishment _____
13. behavior _____
14. quarterback _____
15. disappear _____
16. theory _____
17. wonderful _____
18. biology _____
19. sizzle _____
20. foreign _____
21. transparent _____
22. civilization _____

✳ **Write two ways in which each word may be divided at the end of a writing line.**

23. mosquito   _____mos-quito_____   _____mosqui-to_____
24. ambition   _____   _____
25. boundary   _____   _____
26. gingerbread   _____   _____
27. geography   _____   _____
28. leadership   _____   _____

www.harcourtschoolsupply.com
© Harcourt Achieve Inc. All rights reserved.

Unit 6: Study Skills
Language: Usage and Practice 6, SV 1419027832

Name _____ Date _____

Dictionary: Definitions and Parts of Speech

- A dictionary lists the **definitions** of each entry word. Many words have more than one definition. Usually, the most commonly used definition is given first. Sometimes a definition is followed by a sentence showing a use of the entry word.
- A dictionary also gives the **part of speech** for each entry word. An abbreviation (shown below) stands for each part of speech. Some words can be used as more than one part of speech.
    EXAMPLE: **frost** (frôst) *n.* **1.** frozen moisture. *There was frost on all the leaves.* -*v.* **2.** to cover with frosting. *I'll frost the cake when it's cool.*

 Use the dictionary samples below to answer the questions.

spec-i-fy (spes´ ə fī´) *v.* **1.** to say or tell in an exact way: *Please specify where we should meet you.* **2.** to designate as a specification: *The artist specified brown for the frame.*
spec-i-men (spes´ ə mən) *n.* **1.** a single person or thing that represents the group to which it belongs; example. **2.** a sample of something taken for medical purposes.

speck-le (spek´ əl) *n.* a small speck or mark. -*v.* to mark with speckles.
spec-tac-u-lar (spek tak´ yə lər) *adj.* relating to, or like a spectacle. -*n.* an elaborate show. —spec tac' u lar ly, *adv.*

n.	noun
pron.	pronoun
v.	verb
adj.	adjective
adv.	adverb
prep.	preposition

1. Which word can be used as either a noun or a verb? _____

2. Which word can be used only as a verb? _____

3. Which word can be used only as a noun? _____

4. Which word can be used either as a noun or as an adjective? _____

5. Write a sentence using the first definition of spectacular. _____

6. Write a sentence using the first definition of specify. _____

7. Write a sentence using speckle as a verb. _____

8. Use the second definition of specimen in a sentence. _____

9. Which word shows an adverb form? _____

10. Which word shows two definitions used as a noun? _____

Name _____   Date _____

Dictionary: Word Origins

- An **etymology** is the origin and development of a word.
- Many dictionary entries include etymologies. The etymology is usually enclosed in brackets [ ].
    EXAMPLE: **knit** [ME *knitten* < OE *cnyttan*, to knot]
    The word *knit* comes from the Middle English word *knitten*, which came from the Old English word *cnyttan*, meaning "to tie in a knot."

 Use these dictionary entries to answer the questions.

cam-pus (kam´ pəs) *n.* the grounds and buildings of a school or university. [Latin *campus*, meaning field, perhaps because most colleges used to be in the country.]
chaise longue (shāz lônj´) *n.* a chair with a long seat that supports the sitter's outstretched legs. [French *chaise*, chair + *longue*, long.]
gar-de-nia (gär dēn´ yə) *n.* a fragrant yellow or white flower from an evergreen shrub or tree. [Modern Latin *Gardenia*, from Alexander *Garden*, 1730–1791, U.S. scientist who studied plants.]

pas-teur-ize (pas´ chə rīz) *v.* to heat food to a high temperature in order to destroy harmful bacteria. [From Louis *Pasteur*, inventor of the process.]
rent (rent) *n.* a regular payment for the use of property. [Old French *rente*, meaning taxes.]
ut-ter (ut´ ər) *v.* to express; make known; put forth. [From Middle English or Dutch, *utteren*, literally, out.]
wam-pum (wom´ pəm) *n.* small beads made from shells and used for money or jewelry. [Short for Algonquin *wampompeag*, meaning strings of money.]

1. Which word comes from an Algonquin word? _____

2. What does the Algonquin word mean? _____

3. Which word was formed from the name of an inventor? _____

4. Which word comes from French words? _____

5. What do the French words *chaise* and *longue* mean? _____

6. Which words were formed from the names of scientists? _____

7. Which word is short for the word *wampompeag*? _____

8. Which words come from Latin words? _____

9. Which word comes from a Middle English word? _____

10. What does the French word *rente* mean? _____

11. Which word comes from two languages? _____

12. What does the word *utteren* mean? _____

13. What does the Latin word *campus* mean? _____

14. Which word is the name of a flower? _____

15. Which word names a piece of furniture? _____

Name _____ Date _____

Using the Library

- Nonfiction books on library shelves are arranged by **call numbers**.
- Each book is assigned a number from 000 to 999, according to its subject matter.
- The main subject groups for call numbers are as follows:

000–099 Reference	500–599 Science and Math
100–199 Philosophy	600–699 Technology
200–299 Religion	700–799 The Arts
300–399 Social Sciences	800–899 Literature
400–499 Languages	900–999 History and Geography

 Write the call number group in which you would find each book.

1. *A Guide to Electronics in a New Age* _____
2. *A Traveler's Handbook of Everyday German* _____
3. *World Almanac and Book of Facts* _____
4. *A History of the Roman Empire* _____
5. *The Modern Philosophers* _____
6. *Religions of the World* _____
7. *Solving Word Problems in Mathematics* _____
8. *Folktales of Norway* _____
9. *Painting with Watercolors* _____
10. *People in Society* _____
11. *Learn Spanish in Seven Days* _____
12. *Science Experiments for the Beginner* _____
13. *Technology in a New Century* _____
14. *Funny Poems for a Rainy Day* _____
15. *The Continent of Africa* _____

Write the titles of three of your favorite nonfiction books. Write the call number group beside each title.

16. _____
17. _____
18. _____

Name _____   Date _____

Using an Encyclopedia

- An **encyclopedia** is a reference book that contains articles on many different subjects.
- The articles are arranged alphabetically in volumes. Each volume is marked to show which articles are inside.
- Guide words are used to show the first topic on each page.
- At the end of most articles, there is a listing of cross-references to related topics for the reader to investigate.

 Read each sample encyclopedia entry below. Then refer to each to answer the questions that follow.

> **BIRDSEYE**, Clarence (1886–1956) was an American food expert and inventor. Birdseye was born in Brooklyn, N.Y., and educated at Amherst College. He is best known for developing methods of preserving foods and for marketing quick-frozen foods. He also worked on lighting technology, wood-pulping methods, and heating processes. *See also* FOOD PROCESSING.

1. Whom is the article about? _____

2. When did he live? _____

3. Where did he go to college? _____

4. What is he best known for? _____

5. What else did he work on? _____

6. What other article in the encyclopedia is related to the subject? _____

> **FOOD PROCESSING** is a method by which food is protected from spoiling for future use. Preserved food should look, taste, and feel like the original food. Many methods are used today to preserve food.
> **Canning** In this process, food is sterilized through heat treatments and sealed in airtight containers. Canned food stored in the cold of Antarctica was preserved for 50 years. This would not be true of canned food stored in hot climates.
> **Freezing** The freezing process was not widely used until the late 19th century. Freezing does not kill all types of bacteria, and care must be taken that foods are not thawed and refrozen. Freezing has the advantage of keeping food looking more like the fresh product than canning does.

7. Why do you think this cross-reference is included in the article about Birdseye?

_____

_____

8. Does the above cross-reference mention Clarence Birdseye? _____

Name _____ Date _____

Finding an Encyclopedia Article

When looking for an article in the encyclopedia:
- Always look up the last name of a person.
    EXAMPLE: To find an article on Helen Keller, look under Keller.
- Look up the first word in the name of a city, state, or country.
    EXAMPLE: To find an article on Puerto Rico, look under Puerto.
- Look up the most specific word in the name of a geographical location.
    EXAMPLE: To find an article on Lake Erie, look under Erie.
- Look up the most significant word in the name of a general topic.
    EXAMPLE: To find an article on neon lamps, look under neon.

 The example below shows how the volumes of a particular encyclopedia are marked to indicate the alphabetical range of the articles they cover. Write the number of the volume in which you would find each article.

A	B	C–CH	CI–CZ	D	E	F	G	H	I–J	K	L
1	2	3	4	5	6	7	8	9	10	11	12
M	N	O	P	Q–R	S–SH	SI–SZ	T	U–V	W–X–Y–Z		
13	14	15	16	17	18	19	20	21	22		

1. camping _____
2. North Dakota _____
3. Jonathan Swift _____
4. giant panda _____
5. Nova Scotia _____
6. John F. Kennedy _____
7. Mount Kilimanjaro _____
8. sand flea _____
9. New Guinea _____
10. Babe Ruth _____
11. Caspian Sea _____
12. Smith College _____
13. Victor Hugo _____
14. elementary school _____
15. Lake Ontario _____

 Look up the following articles in an encyclopedia. Write a cross-reference for each article.

16. bee _____
17. X-ray _____
18. atom _____
19. music _____
20. Georgia _____
21. space travel _____
22. Susan B. Anthony _____
23. cartoon _____

 Choose a person who interests you and find the entry for that person in an encyclopedia. Then answer the questions below.

24. Who is the person you've chosen? _____
25. When did this person live? _____
26. What made this person famous? _____
27. What encyclopedia did you use? _____

Name _____ Date _____

Choosing Reference Sources

- Use a dictionary to find the definitions and pronunciations of words, suggestions for word usage, and etymologies.
- Use an encyclopedia to find articles about many different people, places, and other subjects. Also use an encyclopedia to find references to related topics.
- Use an atlas to find maps and other information about geographical locations.

 Write encyclopedia, dictionary, or atlas to show which source you would use to find the following information. Some topics might be found in more than one source.

1. the pronunciation of the word measure _____
2. the location of Yellowstone National Park _____
3. the care and feeding of a dog _____
4. the distance between Rome and Naples _____
5. jewelry throughout the ages _____
6. planning a vegetable garden _____
7. the meaning of the word federal _____
8. the etymology of the word consider _____
9. the early life of Abraham Lincoln _____
10. the states through which the Mississippi River flows _____
11. how volcanoes form _____
12. a definition of the word ape _____
13. the rivers and mountains of Canada _____
14. how paper is made _____
15. the location of the border between Vermont and New Hampshire _____
16. the history of kite making _____
17. the pronunciation of the word particular _____
18. the names of lakes in Northern California _____
19. the meanings of the homographs of bow _____
20. methods of scoring in football _____

Name _____   Date _____

Unit 6 Test

Refer to the dictionary samples to answer the questions that follow. Darken the circle by the best answer.

leav-en (lev´ən) *n.* **1.** a substance that causes dough to rise. **2.** a small piece of such dough put aside to be used for causing other dough to rise. *-v.* to cause dough to rise. [Middle English, from Old French, from Latin *levein.*]
left (left) *adj.* toward the side of the body that is westward when facing north. *-n.* that which is on the left. *-adv.* toward the left. [Middle English *lift*, from Old English *lyft*, weak.]

let (let) *v.* **1.** to permit or allow: *Did he let you go?* **2.** to allow to pass through: *I let the bird out of its cage.* **3.** to make; cause: *They'll let us know.* **4.** to rent. [Old English *laeten*, to allow.]

1. Which word has two syllables?
   Ⓐ leaven   Ⓒ let
   Ⓑ left   Ⓓ none of the above

2. Which pair of words could be guide words for the entries above?
   Ⓐ length / liar   Ⓒ leaf / level
   Ⓑ lay / lean   Ⓓ none of the above

3. Which word has the most definitions?
   Ⓐ leaven   Ⓒ left
   Ⓑ let   Ⓓ none of the above

4. As which part of speech can <u>left</u> not be used?
   Ⓐ pronoun   Ⓒ adverb
   Ⓑ adjective   Ⓓ none of the above

5. Which word originally meant "weak"?
   Ⓐ let   Ⓒ leaven
   Ⓑ left   Ⓓ none of the above

6. From how many other languages did <u>leaven</u> come?
   Ⓐ two   Ⓒ four
   Ⓑ three   Ⓓ none of the above

Darken the circle by the reference you would use to find the following information.

7. the distance from Kansas City to Chicago
   Ⓐ dictionary   Ⓒ atlas
   Ⓑ encyclopedia   Ⓓ none of the above

8. information about mural painting
   Ⓐ dictionary   Ⓒ atlas
   Ⓑ encyclopedia   Ⓓ none of the above

9. the etymology of the word <u>define</u>
   Ⓐ dictionary   Ⓒ atlas
   Ⓑ encyclopedia   Ⓓ none of the above

10. the history of doll collecting
    Ⓐ dictionary   Ⓒ atlas
    Ⓑ encyclopedia   Ⓓ none of the above

11. the state in which Kitty Hawk is located
    Ⓐ dictionary   Ⓒ atlas
    Ⓑ encyclopedia   Ⓓ none of the above

12. the definition of the word <u>technology</u>
    Ⓐ dictionary   Ⓒ atlas
    Ⓑ encyclopedia   Ⓓ none of the above

13. the pronunciation of the word <u>pneumonia</u>
    Ⓐ dictionary   Ⓒ atlas
    Ⓑ encyclopedia   Ⓓ none of the above

14. how a bill is passed in Congress
    Ⓐ dictionary   Ⓒ atlas
    Ⓑ encyclopedia   Ⓓ none of the above

15. the states the Missouri River passes through
    Ⓐ dictionary   Ⓒ atlas
    Ⓑ encyclopedia   Ⓓ none of the above

16. what the local weather will be today
    Ⓐ dictionary   Ⓒ atlas
    Ⓑ encyclopedia   Ⓓ none of the above

Name _____ Date _____

Unit 6 Test, p. 2

Write the call number group in which you would find each book.

> 000–099 Reference
> 100–199 Philosophy
> 200–299 Religion
> 300–399 Social Sciences
> 400–499 Languages
> 500–599 Science and Math
> 600–699 Technology
> 700–799 The Arts
> 800–899 Literature
> 900–999 History and Geography

17. *The Encyclopedia of the American Indian* _____

18. *Plants of the American Southwest* _____

19. *Major Religions of the World* _____

20. *Going West on the Oregon Trail* _____

Use the sample encyclopedia article to answer the questions. Darken the circle by the correct choice.

> **WATER** is a liquid. Like air (oxygen), water is necessary for all living things. A person can live only a few days without water. Water is lost from the body every day and must be replaced. Drinking and eating replace water. About 60 percent of a person's body weight is water. *See also* OXYGEN.

21. What is this article about? _____

22. How much of a person's body is water? _____

23. How is water in the body replaced? _____

24. What other subject could you look under to get more information? _____

Darken the circle by the volume in an encyclopedia where each article would be found.

A	B	C–CH	CI–CZ	D	E	F	G	H	I–J	K	L
1	2	3	4	5	6	7	8	9	10	11	12
M	N	O	P	Q–R	S–SH	SI–SZ	T	U–V	W–X–Y–Z		
13	14	15	16	17	18	19	20	21	22		

25. North Carolina
    - Ⓐ 3
    - Ⓑ 4
    - Ⓒ 13
    - Ⓓ 14

26. Mahatma Gandhi
    - Ⓐ 8
    - Ⓑ 9
    - Ⓒ 13
    - Ⓓ 14

27. Olympic Games
    - Ⓐ 8
    - Ⓑ 15
    - Ⓒ 18
    - Ⓓ 19

28. country music
    - Ⓐ 3
    - Ⓑ 4
    - Ⓒ 13
    - Ⓓ 22

Answer Key

Assessment
Pages 7–10
1. A
2. H
3. S
4. H
5. can
6. S
7. C
8. P
9. P
10. can not
11. they will
12. curious
13. b

The words in bold should be circled.
14. IN, **Who**, is going
15. E, **I**, feel
16. IM, **(You)**, do worry
17. D, **It**, is
18. CP
19. CS
20. RO
21. I
22. CS
23. Underline: officer, person. Circle: Paul, Judge Hawkins.
24. friend's
25. Underline: a baseball legend. Circle: Nolan Ryan.
26. Underline: will discover. Circle: will.
27. past
28. future
29. present
30. flew, went
31. drank, threw
32. froze, broke

The words in bold should be circled.
33. SP, **You**
34. IP, **Nobody**
35. PP, **her**
36. OP, **us**
37. adjective
38. adverb
39. adverb
40. adjective
41. Can
42. learn
43. set
44. laid
45. doesn't
46. The words in bold should be circled. You can wait either in the car or outside the door.

Letter:
832 Southern Star
Helena, MT 95097
Aug. 27, 2007
Dear Edward,
 I have the information you wanted. Did you ever think I'd get it to you this quickly? Well, it's time I surprised you. Here's what you should bring: six cartons of orange juice, forty-five paper cups, and three bags of ice. What a breakfast party this will be!
Your friend,
Bill

47. Answers will vary.
48. 5
49. 1
50. 6
51. 2
52. 3
53. 4
54. title
55. noun
56. after
57. care/carrot
58. 2
59. car-pet
60. atlas or encyclopedia
61. encyclopedia
62. dictionary
63. atlas or encyclopedia
64. dictionary
65. encyclopedia

Unit 1
Page 11
1.–12. Synonyms will vary.
13. begin
14. fall
15. sick
16. tired
17. close
18.–29. Antonyms will vary.
30. heavy
31. late
32. kind
33. empty
34. found

Page 12
1. beach
2. deer
3. weigh
4. pane
5. to, to, two
6. knew, new
7. their
8. ate, eight
9. sea
10. Ring
11. here
12. write, right
13. read
14. buy, by
15. tale
16. haul
17. through
18. week
19. they're or their
20. herd
21. hear
22. buy or bye
23. pain
24. heel or he'll
25. blue
26. flour
27. stare
28. pail
29. wring
30. sore
31. sail
32. one
33. I'll or isle
34. road or rowed
35. meat or mete
36. hour
37. see
38. write or rite
39. piece
40. know
41. great
42. weigh or whey
43. sent or scent
44. do or due
45. fourth

Page 13
1. checks
2. interest
3. vault
4. interest
5. vault
6. checks
7.–11. Sentences will vary.
7. a
8. a
9. a
10. a
11. b

Page 14
1.–5. Definitions will vary.
1. impractical
2. misbehave
3. uneasy
4. nonviolent
5. unusual
6.–17. Meanings will vary.
6. un
7. dis
8. dis
9. mis
10. pre
11. re
12. mis
13. im
14. non
15. un
16. in
17. pre

Page 15
1.–5. Definitions will vary.
1. mountainous
2. helpful
3. snowy
4. national
5. knowledgeable
6.–17. Meanings will vary.
6. able
7. less
8. ous
9. able
10. ous
11. able
12. ous
13. ful
14. y
15. less
16. al
17. al

Page 16
1. they're, they are
2. won't, will not
3. There's, There is
4. That's, That is; shouldn't, should not
5. weren't, were not
6. doesn't, does not
7. can't, cannot; it's, it is
8. they've, they have; they'll, they will
9. It's, It is; aren't, are not
10. you'd, you would
11. I have, I've; I would, I'd
12. It is, It's; what is, what's
13. I will, I'll
14. does not, doesn't

Page 17
1.–8. Answers will vary.
9. forehead
10. haircut
11. everywhere
12. newsstand
13. loudspeaker
14. everything

Page 18
1. wonderful
2. Brave
3. fascinating
4. hilarious
5. smile
6. cheap

7. soggy
8. nagged
9. silly
10. smirk
11. frightened
12. antique
13. slender
14. thrifty
15. parade
16. disaster
17. sip
18. starving
19. filthy

Page 19
1. j   5. e   9. b
2. i   6. f   10. c
3. h   7. d
4. a   8. g
Meanings will vary.
11. in hot water
12. beside themselves
13. fly off the handle
14. shaken up
15. talk turkey

Unit 1 Test
Pages 20–21
1. D   13. D   25. C
2. A   14. A   26. B
3. B   15. C   27. B
4. C   16. B   28. D
5. B   17. D   29. B
6. C   18. D   30. A
7. D   19. C   31. C
8. A   20. A   32. B
9. C   21. A   33. A
10. B 22. D   34. C
11. C 23. B   35. B
12. B 24. C   36. B

Unit 2
Page 22
S should precede the following sentences, and students should end each with a period: 2, 5, 7, 9, 10, 11, 12, 13, 16, 19, 20, 21, 22, 24, 28, 29.

Page 23
1. IN   11. D   21. IN
2. IN   12. D   22. D
3. D   13. IN 23. D
4. D   14. D   24. IN
5. D   15. IN 25. D
6. IN   16. D   26. IN
7. D   17. D   27. IN
8. D   18. IN 28. D
9. IN   19. D
10. IN 20. IN

Page 24
1. IM   15. E
2. IM   16. E
3. E   17. E
4. IM   18. IM
5. E   19. IM
6. IM or E 20. E
7. IM   21. E
8. IM   22. IM
9. IM   23. E
10. IM   24. IM
11. E   25. IM
12. IM   26. IM
13. E   27. E
14. E   28. E

Page 25
1. Bees / fly.
2. Trains / whistle.
3. artist / drew
4. wind / blew
5. grandmother / made
6. We / surely
7. cookies / are
8. letter / came
9. They / rent
10. Jennifer / is
11. team / won
12. band / played
13. sky / is
14. auctioneer / was
15. lightning / startled
16. wind / howled
17. dog / followed
18. apartment / is
19. We / have
20. team / deserves
21. rangers / fought
22. friend / taught
23. stars / make
24. airplane / was
25. children / waded
26. Park / is
27. weather / is
28. trees / were

Page 26
Words in bold print should be underlined twice.
1. clap of thunder / **frightened**
2. snow / **covered**
3. We / **drove**
4. students / **are making**
5. class / **read**
6. women / **were talking**
7. album / **has**
8. We / **are furnishing**
9. trees on that lawn / **are**
10. Americans / **are working**
11. manager / **read**
12. Terrill / **brought**
13. We / **opened**
14. mechanics / **worked**
15. butterflies / **fluttered**
16. child / **spoke**
17. We / **found**
18. part of the program / **is**
19. person / **is working**
20. Sheryl / **swam**
21. program / **will begin**
22. handle of this basket / **is**
23. clock in the tower / **strikes**
24. farmhouse on that road / **belongs**
25. game of the season / **will be played**

Page 27
Sentences 1, 3, 4, 5, 6, 8, 9, 11, and 12 are in inverted order.
1. falls / the
2. tree / are
3. rolled / the
4. marched / the
5. are / many
6. ran / the
7. He / hit
8. hiked / the
9. is / the
10. fish / jumped
11. came / the
12. came / the
13. The mist falls lightly.
14. The rocks rolled over and over.
15. The band marched down the street.
16. Many birds are near the ocean.
17. The kitten ran right under the chair.
18. The campers hiked along the ridge.
19. The stream is underground.
20. The trucks came over the hill.
21. The rainbow came out.

Page 28
Sentences 1, 2, 3, 4, 6, 7, 8, and 9 have compound subjects.
1. English settlers and Spanish settlers / came
2. Trees and bushes / were
3. The fierce winds and the cold temperatures / made
4. The settlers and Native Americans / became
5. Native Americans / helped
6. Potatoes and corn / were
7. English settlers and Spanish settlers / had
8. Peanuts and sunflower seeds / are
9. Lima beans and corn / are
10. Zucchini / is
11. Native Americans / also
12. Gold and silver from the New World were sent to Spain.
13. France and the Netherlands staked claims in the Americas in the 1500s and 1600s.
14. John Cabot and Henry Hudson explored areas of the Americas.
15. Sentences will vary.

Page 29
Sentences 2, 3, 4, 6, 8, 9, 11, and 12 have compound predicates.
1. students / organized
2. They / discussed
3. They / wrote
4. invitations / were
5. families / responded
6. students / bought
7. families / bought
8. students / packed
9. families / brought
10. Everyone / participated
11. They / ran
12. Everyone / packed
13. Carrie heard and memorized the music.
14. Keith picked up and loaded the newspapers into his car.
15. Lance studied and wrote down the names of the states.
16. Sentences will vary.

Page 30
Sentences 1, 3, 5, and 6 are simple. Sentences 2 and 4 are compound.
1. world / are
2. Earth / is, it / is
3. world / are
4. We / cannot, we / cannot
5. drink / comes

6. water / is
7. The Pacific Ocean is the largest ocean in the world, and it covers more area than all of Earth's land put together.
8. Bodies of salt water that are smaller than oceans are called seas, gulfs, or bays, and these bodies of water are often encircled by land.
9. Seas, gulfs, and bays are joined to the oceans, and they vary in size and depth.
10. The Mediterranean is one of Earth's largest seas, and it is almost entirely encircled by the southern part of Europe, the northern part of Africa, and the western part of Asia.

Page 31
Sentences may vary.
1. In 1860, the Pony Express started in St. Joseph, Missouri. The route began where the railroads ended.
2. People in the West wanted faster mail service. The mail took six weeks by boat.
3. Mail sent by stagecoach took about 21 days. The Pony Express averaged ten days.
4. The Pony Express used a relay system. Riders and horses were switched at 157 places along the way to Sacramento, California.
5. Because teenagers weighed less than adults, most of the riders were teenagers. The horses could run faster carrying them.
6. Riders had to cross raging rivers. The mountains were another barrier.

Page 32
Expanded sentences will vary.

Unit 2 Test
Pages 33–34
1. B
2. A
3. D
4. C
5. B
6. A
7. A
8. C
9. D
10. B
11. A
12. B
13. C
14. D
15. C
16. A
17. A
18. C
19. B
20. D
21. C
22. A
23. B
24. C
25. A
26. B
27. C
28. A
29. A
30. C
31. C
32. A

Unit 3
Page 35
1.–5. Answers will vary.
6. Alaska; gold; silver; copper; oil
7. Chocolate; beans; tree; tropics
8. distance; Texas; distance; Chicago; New York
9. men; women; horses; parade
10. city; California; San Diego
11. Alexander Graham Bell; inventor; telephone; Edinburgh; Scotland
12. Jack; Diane; plane; London; Buckingham Palace
13. animals; piranhas; alligators; anacondas; sloths; Amazon River Basin
14. tarantula; type; spider
15. Maya; people; Mexico; Central America

Pages 36–37
1.–40. Answers will vary. Check that students' answers fulfill the assignment.
41. timber; oak; furniture; bridges; ships
42. painter; jeweler; farmer; engineer; inventor
43. crops; sugar; tobacco; coffee; fruits
44. groves; nuts; part
45. rivers; beaches
46. bridge; world
47. foods; lamb; fish; olives; cheese
48. road; tunnel; base; tree
49. civilizations; gold; ornaments
50. lakes
51. tree; blossoms; fruits
52. center
53. trees; turpentine; tar; resin; timber; oils
54. amount; coffee
55. pelican; penguin; flamingo; birds
56. trip; space; danger
57. Brazil
58. William Penn; Pennsylvania
59. Elm Grove Library
60. Commander Byrd; North Pole
61. Dr. Jeanne Spurlock; Howard University College of Medicine
62. Europe; Asia
63. Colombia
64. Kilimanjaro; Africa
65. Navajo
66. Bena; Carlos; Sam; Teri
67. Thomas Jefferson; United States
68. Lake Michigan
69. Quebec; North America
70. Paul Revere
71. India
72. Sears Tower; Chicago

Pages 38–39
1. newspapers
2. guesses
3. towns
4. valleys
5. bodies
6. stories
7. bushes
8. offices
9. taxes
10. toys
11. bosses
12. schools
13. days
14. copies
15. authors
16. porches
17. pennies
18. dresses
19. bridges
20. brushes
21. counties
22. foxes
23. books
24. lunches
25. countries
26. knives
27. loaves
28. halves
29. mice
30. feet
31. geese
32. hooves
33. moose
34. lives
35. tomatoes
36. teeth
37. pianos
38. feet
39. sheep
40. chimneys
41. cities
42. leaves
43. Mosquitoes
44. nickels
45. friends
46. desks
47. benches

Pages 40–41
1. girl's
2. child's
3. women's
4. children's
5. John's
6. baby's
7. boys'
8. teacher's
9. Dr. Ray's
10. ladies'
11. brother's
12. soldier's
13. men's
14. aunt's
15. Ms. Jones's
16. Jim's cap
17. Kathy's wrench
18. baby's smile
19. friend's car
20. Kim's new shoes
21. dog's collar
22. Frank's golf clubs
23. runners' shoes
24. parents' friends
25. editor's opinion
26. children's lunches
27. Kyle's coat
28. teacher's assignment
29. company's
30. dog's
31. women's
32. Doug's
33. David's
34. cat's
35. Kurt's
36. Men's
37. squirrel's
38. brother's
39. child's
40. calf's
41. baby's
42. teachers'
43. Alex's
44. deer's

45. Stacy's
46. country's
47. robins'
48. person's
49. sister's
50. children's
51. neighbors'
52. class's
53. boys'
54. designer's
55. horse's

Page 42
Students should circle the phrases in bold.
1. **my father's older brother,** Henry
2. **the Missouri Pacific,** train
3. **the location of the main station,** Seattle
4. **its main cargo,** Coal and lumber
5. **our uncle,** Henry
6. **his nephews,** us
7. **his brother,** father
8. **his sister-in-law,** mother
9. **his wife,** Aunt Emma
10. **Todd and Elizabeth,** cousins
11.–16. Sentences will vary.

Page 43
1. are
2. wrote
3. Check
4. have
5. is
6. reached
7. won
8. trains
9. has
10. are
11. remember
12. bought
13. is
14. followed
15. whistled
16. watches
17. scored
18. won
19. is
20. lies
21. set
22. Answer
23. explained
24. worked
25. has
26. plays
27. Brush
28. whirled
29. arrived
30. is

Page 44
1. were held
2. invented
3. was
4. was
5. built
6. will arrive
7. was
8. has made
9. covered
10. have ridden
11. is molding
12. spent
13. are posted
14. has found
15. is going
16. have trimmed
17. exports
18. is reading
19. helped
20. was discovered
21. was called
22. are planning
23. has howled
24. have arrived
25. have written
26. can name
27. received
28. was printed
29. are working
30. was painted

Page 45
Students should circle the words in bold.
1. **have** begun
2. **will** rake
3. **must** sweep
4. **will** pull
5. **may** prepare
6. **should** wash
7. **would** make
8. **is** working
9. **has** sprayed
10. **must** close
11. **would** enjoy
12. **might** finish
13.–20. Sentences will vary.

Page 46
Students should circle the words in bold.
1. **will be** given
2. **have been** studying
3. **may be** forming
4. **should be** reviewing
5. **Are** joining
6. **May** meet
7. **should have** known
8. **have** been
9. **have been** looking
10. **would have** met
11. **has been** delayed
12. **Would** prefer
13. **had been** enjoying
14. **have been** waiting
15. **had** been
16. **Will be** swimming
17. **must have been** splashing
18. **Could** take
19.–20. Statements will vary.
21.–22. Questions will vary.

Page 47
1. Is
2. are
3. is
4. are
5. is
6. are
7. are
8. Are
9. is
10. are
11. were
12. were
13. were
14. were
15. was
16. was
17. was
18. were
19. were
20. was

Page 48
1. works; present
2. care; present
3. play; present
4. threw; past
5. sailed; past
6. ran; past
7. shouted; past
8. listens; present
9. got; past
10. called; past
11. went; past
12. will play; future
13. My little sister followed me everywhere.
14. She came to my friend's house.
15. She rode my bicycle on the grass.

Page 49
1. is walking; walked; (have, has, had) walked
2. is visiting; visited; (have, has, had) visited
3. is watching; watched; (have, has, had) watched
4. is following; followed; (have, has, had) followed
5. is jumping; jumped; (have, has, had) jumped
6. is talking; talked; (have, has, had) talked
7. is adding; added; (have, has, had) added
8. is learning; learned; (have, has, had) learned
9. is painting; painted; (have, has, had) painted
10. is planting; planted; (have, has, had) planted
11. is working; worked; (have, has, had) worked
12. is dividing; divided; (have, has, had) divided
13. is missing; missed; (have, has, had) missed
14. is scoring; scored; (have, has, had) scored
15. is calling; called; (have, has, had) called
16. is collecting; collected; (have, has, had) collected

Page 50
1. saw
2. came
3. did
4. saw
5. did
6. came
7. done
8. come
9. seen
10. done
11. came
12. seen
13. come
14. seen
15. came
16. saw
17. did
18. come
19. saw
20. done
21. came
22. did
23. come
24. saw
25. come
26. seen
27. did
28. came
29. saw
30. done

Page 51
1. eaten
2. drank
3. ate
4. drunk
5. ate
6. drank
7. eaten
8. drunk
9. ate
10. drank
11. ate
12. drank
13. eaten
14. drunk
15. eaten
16. drank
17. eaten
18. drunk
19. ate
20. drunk
21. drank
22. eaten
23. drank
24. eaten
25. drunk
26. ate

Page 52
1. sung
2. rung
3. sang
4. rung
5. sang

6. rang
7. sang
8. rang
9. sung
10. rang
11. sung
12. rung
13. sang; sung
14. rung
15. sang
16. rung
17. rung
18. sang
19. sung
20. rang
21. rung
22. sang
23. rang
24. sung
25. rang
26. sang

Page 53
1. spoken
2. frozen
3. broke
4. spoken
5. chosen
6. broken
7. spoken
8. froze
9. chose
10. broken
11. spoke
12. froze
13. broken
14. chose
15. spoke
16. frozen
17. frozen
18. broken
19. chosen
20. spoke
21. chosen
22. chose
23. broken
24. spoke
25. frozen
26. spoken

Page 54
1. known
2. grew
3. thrown
4. known
5. grown
6. thrown
7. grown
8. knew
9. grown
10. known
11. thrown
12. grew
13. threw
14. grown
15. knew
16. threw
17. known
18. grew
19.–24. Sentences will vary.

Page 55
1. flew
2. blown
3. flown
4. blew
5. blew
6. flown
7. flew
8. blown
9. flew
10. blown
11. flown
12. blown
13. flew
14. blown
15. flown
16. blew
17. flown
18. blew
19. flew
20. blown
21. flew
22. blew
23. flown
24.–27. Sentences will vary.

Page 56
1. took
2. written
3. taken
4. wrote
5. took
6. written
7. took
8. wrote
9. taken
10. written
11. took
12. written
13. took
14. wrote
15. wrote
16. taken
17. written
18. taken
19. wrote
20. taken
21. wrote
22. wrote
23. took
24. wrote
25. took

Page 57
1. given
2. gone
3. gave
4. went
5. gave
6. gone
7. gave
8. gone
9. gave
10. gone
11. given
12. went
13. given
14. gone
15. given
16. gone
17. went
18. given
19. gone
20. given
21. gone
22. given
23. gone
24. gave
25. went
26. given

Page 58
1. her
2. his
3. their
4. her
5. their
6. his
7. his
8. its
9. their
10. their
11. its
12. his
13. its
14. its
15. her
16. her
17. his
18. its
19. his
20. your
21. his
22. their
23. her
24. his
25. his
26. their

Page 59
1. Everyone
2. somebody
3. Anything
4. Something
5. Everybody
6. No one
7. anyone
8. Both
9. Nothing
10. anybody
11. Someone
12. Everybody
13. Each
14. Some
15. Several
16. No one
17. Everyone
18. Nobody
19. Everything
20. anything
21.–28. Pronouns will vary.

Page 60
1. I
2. She
3. I
4. She
5. I
6. He
7. he
8. She; I
9. I
10. He
11. we
12. They
13. I
14. It
15. You
16. He
17. I
18. She
19. We
20. They
21. she
22. I
23. We
24. we
25. He
26. She
27. I

Page 61
1. me
2. me
3. her
4. us
5. her
6. them
7. me
8. him
9. him
10. her
11. me
12. us
13. us
14. us
15. them
16. me
17. us
18. him
19. me
20. him
21. them
22. us
23. her
24. him
25. them
26. her
27. us

Page 62
1. I
2. she
3. we
4. they
5. she
6. he
7. I
8. she
9. he
10. she
11. he
12. they
13. he
14. she
15. we
16. I
17. they
18. she
19. they
20. she
21. they
22. he
23. she
24. she
25. he
26. she

Page 63
1. Who
2. Who
3. Whom
4. Who
5. Who
6. Who
7. Whom
8. Whom
9. Whom
10. Whom
11. Who
12. Whom
13. Who
14. Who
15. Whom
16. Who
17. Who
18. Whom
19. Who
20. Whom
21. Who

Page 64
1. He; us
2. you
3. we
4. we
5. you; him
6. She; them
7. He; me
8. Who; you
9. I; them
10. me; she
11. they; us
12. I; her
13. you; him
14. you; me; I
15. her; him
16. she; them
17. I; you
18. He; I
19. They; me
20. Who
21. whom; I
22. I; it; me
23. She; me
24. They; us
25. We; he
26. us
27. you; I
28. You; you; it
29. they; us
30. I; them
31. us
32. Who
33. She; I; you
34. We; them

Page 65
1. I
2. he
3. I
4. them
5. me
6. me
7. her
8. Who
9. I
10. us
11. whom
12. me
13. our
14. me
15. her
16. us
17. she
18. Who
19. their
20. me
21. whom
22. her
23. us
24. his
25. We
26. me
27. Who
28. I
29. them
30. I; his
31. whom
32. she
33. she
34. We

Page 66
Adjectives will vary.

Page 67
1. a
2. a
3. a
4. an
5. a
6. an
7. a
8. a
9. a
10. an
11. an
12. an
13. a
14. an
15. a
16. an
17. an
18. an
19. an
20. a
21. an
22. a
23. an
24. a
25. an
26. an
27. an
28. a
29. a
30. a
31. an
32. an
33. a
34. a
35. a
36. a
37. an
38. an
39. an
40. a
41. a
42. an
43. a
44. an
45. an
46. an
47. an
48. a
49. an
50. an

Page 68
1. South American
2. African
3. English
4. Mexican
5. French
6. Russian
7. American
8. Roman
9. Alaskan
10. Canadian
11. Norwegian
12. Scottish
13. Irish
14. Chinese
15. Spanish
16. Italian
17. Hawaiian
18. Japanese
19.–28. Sentences will vary.

Page 69
1. those
2. these
3. these
4. that
5. this
6. Those
7. these
8. these
9. those
10. those
11. those
12. those
13. That
14. that
15. These
16. that
17. this
18. This
19.–22. Sentences will vary.

Page 70
1. smoother; smoothest
2. younger, youngest
3. sweeter; sweetest
4. stronger; strongest
5. lazier; laziest
6. greater; greatest
7. kinder, kindest
8. calmer; calmest
9. rougher; roughest
10. narrower; narrowest
11. deeper; deepest
12. shorter; shortest
13. happier; happiest
14. colder; coldest
15. prettier; prettiest

Pages 71–72
1.–8. All comparative forms use more. All superlative forms use most.
9.–16. All comparative forms use less. All superlative forms use least.
17. nearer
18. tallest
19. more helpful
20. younger
21. most difficult
22. better
23. smallest
24. hottest
25. youngest
26. widest
27. older
28. largest
29. most courteous
30. best
31. coldest
32. more studious
33. taller
34. wealthiest
35. fastest
36. more useful
37. most beautiful
38. narrowest
39. larger
40. best
41. worst
42. most famous
43. most beautiful

Pages 73–74
1.–18. Adverbs will vary.
19.–24. Sentences will vary.
25. slowly
26. very; quickly
27. too; early
28. patiently
29. very; cautiously
30. always; here
31. very; rapidly
32. swiftly
33. quietly; ahead
34. very; slowly
35. now
36. everywhere
37. extremely
38. always; distinctly
39. far; underwater
40. here
41. quickly
42. very; fast; especially
43. suddenly
44. softly
45. there
46. too; rapidly
47. there; extremely; very
48. politely
49. too; rapidly
50. extremely; well
51. softly
52. carefully
53. wearily
54. very; carefully
55. eagerly
56. recently
57. everywhere; yesterday
58. dearly
59. before
60. badly

Page 75
1. higher, highest
2. later; latest
3. more slowly; most slowly
4. more clearly; most clearly
5. harder; hardest
6. more quickly; most quickly
7. more beautifully; most beautifully
8. longer; longest

Page 76
1. don't; doesn't
2. doesn't
3. Doesn't
4. Doesn't
5. Doesn't
6. don't
7. Doesn't
8. doesn't
9. doesn't
10. doesn't
11. don't
12. doesn't
13. doesn't
14. don't
15. doesn't
16. doesn't
17. Doesn't
18. doesn't
19. doesn't
20. doesn't
21. Don't
22. doesn't
23. doesn't
24. doesn't
25. don't
26. don't
27. Don't
28. don't

Page 77
1. can
2. can
3. may
4. can
5. can
6. may
7. can
8. can
9. can
10. May
11. teach
12. learn
13. teach
14. learn
15. teach
16. teach
17. teach
18. teach; learn

Page 78
1. sit
2. set
3. sit
4. set
5. Set
6. sits
7. set
8. sat
9. sit
10. sit
11. lay
12. Lie
13. lies
14. laid
15. lay
16. lie
17. Lay
18. laid
19. lie
20. lain

Page 79
1. on
2. from; with
3. through; toward
4. between
5. for
6. about
7. into
8. to
9. across
10. against
11. over; into
12. across
13. among; of
14. beside
15. across; toward
16. behind
17. around
18. on
19. about; in
20. in
21. to
22. into
23. across
24. of; from
25. among
26. After; to
27. of; in

Page 80
Students should circle words in bold.
1. (of the **United States**) (of a great **country**)
2. (into the **station wagon**)
3. (on a clear **night**)
4. (of my **desk**)
5. (through a **tunnel**)
6. (on the bulletin **board**)
7. (of **posters**) (in the **showcase**) (in the **corridor**)
8. (to **Ms. Garza**)
9. (of **Alabama**)
10. (on this antique **sofa**) (from **France**)
11. (of **minerals**)
12. (to Julia's **house**)
13. (with beautiful **wildflowers**)

14. (against the **windowpanes**)
15. (above the **door**)
16. (by my oldest **sister**)
17. (of **grapes**) (from the **vine**)
18. (to the **race**)
19. (of **goats**) (on the **hillside**)
20. (to the **storeroom**)
21. (on the **bridge**)
22. (in **St. Louis**)
23. (of **flowers**) (in the **center**) (of the **table**)
24. (around the **fireplace**)
25. (from the **north**)
26. (over the **fence**)
27. (with the **bone**)
28. (by the narrow **path**)

Page 81
1. to the library; adverb
2. about gardening; adjective
3. in the library; adjective
4. with blue shoes; adjective
5. in the green dress; adjective
6. about the library catalog; adverb
7. for every book; adjective
8. in three groups; adverb
9. in the health section; adverb
10. to the library; adjective
11. with her; adverb
12. at home; adverb
13. in the living room; adjective
14. out the window; adverb
15. by the backyard fence; adjective
16. from last year's garden; adjective
17. near the house; adverb
18. in the summer; adverb

Page 82
1. until
2. and
3. and
4. or
5. or
6. and
7. Neither; nor
8. but
9. and
10. for
11.–20. Conjunctions will vary. Suggested:
11. until
12. or

13. and
14. and; but
15. until
16. and
17. and
18. if
19. and
20. Neither; nor

Page 83
Sentences will vary.

Unit 3 Test
Pages 84–85
1. A	16. B	31. C
2. B	17. B	32. B
3. C	18. A	33. C
4. B	19. C	34. A
5. B	20. A	35. A
6. B	21. C	36. C
7. B	22. B	37. B
8. D	23. C	38. A
9. C	24. A	39. A
10. C	25. B	40. C
11. B	26. C	41. B
12. A	27. C	42. A
13. C	28. A	43. C
14. A	29. B	
15. A	30. B	

Unit 4
Pages 86–88
Students should circle and capitalize the first letter in each of the following words:
1. Haven't
2. The
3. Danielle; How
4. The
5. Bring
6. Who
7. The; My
8. Have
9. I; I've; It; But
10. It's; Is; The; The
11. The; Children's; Hour
12. A; Wrinkle; Time
13. Stand; Me
14. Adam; Road
15. Chasing; Wind
16. Students should rewrite the paragraph and capitalize the first letter in each of the following words: chris, chicago, illinois, greek, canadian, charley, italian, mexican, laurel, japanese, irish, german

Students should circle and capitalize the first letter in each of the following words:

17. Anita; Arizona; New; Mexico; Colorado
18. Brazil; United; States
19. Mark; Twain; Hannibal; Missouri
20. Martin; Luther; King
21. Solomon; Islands
22. North; Sea; English; Channel; Strait; Dover
23. Sam; Houston; Tennessee; Lexington; Virginia
24. St.; Augustine; United; States
25. Nairobi; Kenya
26. Japanese
27. Captain; Cheng; Sergeant; Walters
28. Dr.; Ruth; Banks; Mr.; Juan; Gomez
29. Pres.; Alice; Slater; Mr.; Gerald; Norman
30. Principal; Grissom; Mayor; Hadley
31. Halpern; Judge; Patterson
32. Mrs.; Frank; President; Howell
33. Prof.; Mary; Schneider; Dr.; David; Towne
34. Andrew; England
35. Alan; Howell; Supt.; Joyce; Randall

Students should circle and capitalize the letters that are capitalized in each of the following:

36. Capt. Margaret K. Hansen / Lakeview St. / Phoenix, AZ
37. Jackson School / Wilson Stadium / Tues., Sept. / N. Clark Blvd.
38. Mr. Jonathan Bernt / Telson Rd. / Markham, Ontario
39. Lt. Gary X. Louis / Congress Rd. / Syracuse, NY
40. Thanksgiving / Wed., Nov. / Tues., Nov. / Ms. Evans
41. Gen. David Grimes / N. Hayes St. / Louisville, KY

Pages 89–90
1. .	6. ?	11. ?
2. ?	7. .	12. .
3. ?	8. ?	13. ?
4. .	9. .	14. .
5. .	10. ?	15. .

Paragraph:

Have you ever been to the Olympic Games? If not, have you ever seen them on television? I hope to see them in person someday. The Olympic Games are held every four years in a different country. The games started in ancient Greece, but the games as we now know them date back to 1896. Some of the finest athletes in the world compete for bronze, silver, and gold medals. Can you think of a famous Olympic athlete? What is your favorite Olympic sport? It could be a winter or summer sport because the games are held for each season. One U.S. athlete won seven gold medals in swimming at one Olympics. Can you imagine how excited that athlete must have felt, knowing that he had represented the United States so well? That is the U.S. record to date. However, there will be plenty more chances for that record to be broken.

16. .	22. .	28. !
17. !	23. !	29. ! or .
18. !; .	24. .	30. .
19. .	25. !	31. ! or .
20. .	26. ! or .	
21. !; .	27. .	

Paragraph: (Punctuation may vary.)

The state of Maine in New England is a wonderful place to visit in the summer or winter. Have you ever been there? It is best known for its rocky coastline on the Atlantic Ocean. Visitors often drive along the rugged coast. There are numerous quaint sea towns along the coast that date back to the 1600s. What a long time ago that was! (or .) Mount Katahdin and the northern part of the Appalachian Mountains are ideal places for winter sports, such as downhill and cross-country skiing. If you've never seen a deer or moose, you'd probably see plenty of them while hiking in Acadia National Park. It has over 30,000 acres. (or !) Do you know anything about Maine's local fish? Well, there are many kinds that are native to its rivers and lakes. But Maine is famous for its Atlantic lobsters. Rockport and Rockland are two of the largest cities for lobster fishing. Lobsters from northern Maine are flown all over the world. (or !) Blueberries are another big product of Maine. Have you ever had wild blueberries? Some people consider them to be the best. (or !)

Pages 91–92
Students should place commas after words shown:
1. cotton, corn,
2. softball, races,
3. nail,
4. Alex, Henry, Carmen,
5. fastball,
6. peaches,
7. pine, cedar,
8. running,
9. sport,
10. Limestone, marble, granite, Vermont, New Hampshire,
11. steadily,
12. corn,
13. works,
14. road,
15. replied,
16. said,
17. years,
18. said,
19. picnic,
20. here,
21. said,
22. Alberto,
23. asked,
24. remembered,
25. Hunt,
26. week,
27. Levin, dentist,
28. Oh,
29. Dad,
30. neighbor, Johnson,
31. city,
32. Well,
33. Britney,
34. concert,
35. Otto, friend,
36. Susan,
37. Jeff,
38. No,
39. John,
40. Porter, principal,
41. Yes,
42. husband, Hal,

Paragraph:
I have two friends who are always there for me, and I tell them everything. So it was a surprise to me when Kathy, my oldest friend, said, "Well, when are you moving?" I said, "What do you mean?" She said, "I don't believe you, our dearest friend, wouldn't tell us first what was going on in your life." Marcy, my other friend, said, "I feel the same way. Anna, why on Earth did we have to hear about this from Leroy?" "Marcy and Kathy, I don't know what you're talking about," I said. "Oh, don't be ashamed," said Marcy. "We know you must have some good reason, and we're waiting to hear it." "No, I don't have any reason because I'm not moving," I said. "Leroy, that prankster, must have been trying to play a joke on us," said Kathy.

Page 93
1. "Dan, did you ever play football?" asked Tim.
2. Morris asked, "Why didn't you come in for an interview?"
3. "I have never heard a story," said Laurie, "about a ghost."
4. Selina said, "Yuri, thank you for the present." or "Selina," said Yuri, "thank you for the present."
5. "When do we start on our trip to the mountains?" asked Stan.
6. Our guest said, "You don't know how happy I am to be in your house."
7. My sister said, "Kelly bought those beautiful baskets in Mexico." or "My sister," said Kelly, "bought those beautiful baskets in Mexico."
8. "I'm going to plant the spinach," said Doris, "as soon as I get home."
9. players'
10. baby's
11. isn't
12. It's
13. captain's
14. doesn't
15. Men's

Page 94
1. 8:30
2. Sanchez:
3. books:
4. 6:15
5. Graham:
6. driving-safety, presen-
7. forty-two
8. zip-
9. mother-in-law
10. fifty-eight
11. ear-
12. twenty-one
13. air-conditioning
14. pup-

Unit 4 Test
Pages 95–96
1. C
2. D
3. D
4. B
5. C
6. A
7. A
8. B
9. C
10. A
11. B
12. C
13. A
14. C
15. B
16. C
17. C
18. A
19. C
20. A
21. B
22. B
23. C
24. A
25. A
26. A
27. B
28. B

Unit 5
Page 97
Sentences will vary.

Page 98
Topic sentences will vary.

Page 99
Students should circle numbers 1, 3, 4, 5, 7, 8, 10. Detail sentences will vary.

Page 100
Answers will vary.

Page 101
Answers will vary.

Page 102
Outlines will vary.

Page 103
1. facts
2. diameter
3. Mars

Students should underline the first sentence in each paragraph.

Page 104
Yellowstone National Park is the oldest and largest national park in the United States. It is located partly in northwestern Wyoming, partly in southern Montana, and partly in eastern Idaho. During the summer of 1988, large parts of the park were damaged by fire. A serious lack of rain was part of the reason the fire was so severe. One fire threatened to destroy the park's famous lodge, which is constructed entirely of wood. Fortunately, firefighters' efforts saved the lodge from destruction. Today the forests are slowly recovering from the fires.

Page 105
Check that students have added correct proofreader's marks.

Although Yellowstone National Park is the largest national park in the United States, other national parks are also well-known. Yosemite National Park in California has acres of mountain scenery and miles of hiking trails. One of the world's largest waterfalls can also be found in Yosemite.

Mammoth Cave National Park in Kentucky features a huge underground cave. The cave has over 212 miles of corridors. It also has underground lakes, rivers, and waterfalls. This cave system is estimated to be millions of years old.

Many people are surprised to learn that there are national parks in Alaska and Hawaii. Mount McKinley, the highest mountain in North America, is located in Denali National Park in Alaska. You can travel to Hawaii and visit Hawaii Volcanoes National Park. This park has two active volcanoes, rare plants, and animals.

Pages 106–107
1. Chris Morrow
2. Dear Sir or Madam:
3. 9940 Main Street, Brooklyn, NY 11227
4. April 4, 2007

Letters will vary. Students should circle the addresses.

Unit 5 Test

Pages 108–109
1. C
2. D
3. C
4. A
5. B
6. B
7. D
8. B
9. D
10. B
11. D
12. D
13. C
14. D

Unit 6

Page 110
Students should check the following words:
1. fruit, furnish, gate, gallon, fuzz, galaxy, future
2. muddy, moss, motorcycle, moose, morning, mortal
3. perfume, pick, photo, pest, pillow, pile

Students should number the words as follows:
4. rabbit / remind; 2, 3, 1, 5, 7, 9, 8, 4, 11, 12, 10, 6
5. scent/silent; 3, 8, 9, 11, 12, 1, 10, 7, 6, 4, 2, 5
6. occasion/only; 2, 9, 5, 6, 8, 4, 10, 7, 3, 11, 1, 12

Page 111
1. advertise
2. blunder
3. paradise
4. mischievous
5. concrete
6. microphone
7. incident
8. value
9. bi-cy-cle
10. so-lu-tion
11. cat-e-go-ry
12. pun-ish-ment
13. be-hav-ior
14. quar-ter-back
15. dis-ap-pear
16. the-o-ry
17. won-der-ful
18. bi-ol-o-gy
19. siz-zle
20. for-eign
21. trans-par-ent
22. civ-i-li-za-tion
23. mos-quito, mosqui-to
24. am-bition, ambi-tion
25. bound-ary, bounda-ry
26. ginger-bread, gin-gerbread
27. ge-ography, geog-raphy, geogra-phy
28. leader-ship, lead-ership

Page 112
1. speckle
2. specify
3. specimen
4. spectacular
5.–8. Sentences will vary.
9. spectacular
10. specimen

Page 113
1. wampum
2. strings of money
3. pasteurize
4. chaise longue
5. chair; long
6. gardenia; pasteurize
7. wampum
8. campus, gardenia
9. utter
10. taxes
11. utter
12. out
13. field
14. gardenia
15. chaise longue

Page 114
1. 600–699
2. 400–499
3. 000–099
4. 900–999
5. 100–199
6. 200–299
7. 500–599
8. 800–899
9. 700–799
10. 300–399
11. 400–499
12. 500–599
13. 600–699
14. 800–899
15. 900–999
16.–18. Answers will vary.

Page 115
1. Clarence Birdseye
2. 1886–1956
3. Amherst College
4. developing methods of preserving foods and marketing quick-frozen foods
5. lighting technology, wood-pulping methods, and heating processes
6. food processing
7. Answers will vary.
8. no

Page 116
1. 3
2. 14
3. 19
4. 16
5. 14
6. 11
7. 11
8. 7
9. 14
10. 17
11. 3
12. 19
13. 9
14. 18
15. 15
16.–27. Answers will vary.

Page 117
1. dictionary
2. dictionary, encyclopedia, or atlas
3. encyclopedia
4. atlas
5. encyclopedia
6. encyclopedia
7. dictionary
8. dictionary
9. encyclopedia
10. encyclopedia or atlas
11. encyclopedia
12. dictionary
13. encyclopedia or atlas
14. encyclopedia
15. encyclopedia or atlas
16. encyclopedia
17. dictionary
18. encyclopedia or atlas
19. dictionary
20. encyclopedia

Unit 6 Test

Page 118–119
1. A
2. C
3. B
4. A
5. B
6. B
7. C
8. B
9. A
10. B
11. B or C
12. A
13. A
14. B
15. C or B
16. D
17. 000–099
18. 500–599
19. 200–299
20. 900–999
21. water
22. about 60 percent
23. by drinking and eating
24. oxygen
25. D
26. A
27. B
28. C